SIXTEEN WEEKS TO FADE OUT

SIXTEEN WEEKS TO FADE OUT

A Practical Guide to Screenwriting

Dr. Michael D. Acosta, MFA, Ed.S.

PUBLISHED BY THE UNIVERSITY OF NORTH CAROLINA AT CHAPEL HILL
WRITING FOR THE SCREEN AND STAGE PROGRAM

DOI: https://doi.org/10.5149/9781469674278_Acosta

Library of Congress Cataloging-in-Publication Data
Names: Acosta, Michael D., author.
Title: Sixteen weeks to fade out : a practical guide to
screenwriting / Dr. Michael D. Acosta, MFA, Ed.S.
Description: Chapel Hill : University of North Carolina
at Chapel Hill Writing for the Screen and Stage
Program, [2023]
Identifiers: LCCN 2022051847 | ISBN 9781469674261
(paperback) | ISBN 9781469674278 (open access ebook)
Subjects: LCSH: Motion picture authorship. | Motion
picture plays. | LCGFT: Programmed instructional materials.
Classification: LCC PN1996 .A36 2023 | DDC 400.82—dc24/
eng20221103
LC record available at https://lccn.loc.gov/2022051847

ACKNOWLEDGMENTS

To my ever-growing family who provides ever-lasting stories. Each one is cherished. *Saol an teaghlaigh ar dtús.*

To my students past, present, and future for helping me stay passionate about teaching by never disappointing me with their passion for writing.

To my friend Brandon who taught me to write. *Super genius. Semper fi.*

CONTENTS

FADE IN.

You have an idea for a film, and you only have the semester to complete the first draft. Sixteen weeks until you have to write FADE OUT. This may feel like a gargantuan task. I promise you that it is not unmanageable. Stephen King likes to finish his first drafts within the span of a season, which is three months. Let's say a good average word count for one of his books is one hundred thousand words. That averages 1,250 words per day (five pages) and can be done in eighty days. This allows for weekends off. An average 120-page screenplay has about fifteen thousand words. At Stephen King's pace a script could be completed in eleven days. Cameron Crowe kicked out *Vanilla Sky* in a weekend, and John Hughes wrote *Ferris Bueller's Day Off* in a week. I assure you that your first draft script can be done and with quality in sixteen weeks.

All writers are different. All writers have their own process. Many writers have no idea what their process is. I do not suppose that there is a *one way is best* mentality. What I do posit is that a well-structured screenplay can be scribed in sixteen weeks. If you do the work as described in this text, you may have a screenplay that has all the fundamental pillars of a top-flight film. The caveat I offer is that the longer you work on a story, the better it gets. For me, that means getting a solid structure and functional characters down in a first draft as efficiently as possible, so that I can concentrate on doing all the small, complex things that make scripts into good movies.

Here's another point. In Hollywood having only one thing to sell isn't always the best way forward. Tastes change, genres change, funds change, distribution changes, talent changes, and what was hot three months ago may not work again for several years. I won't say the days of pitches are over, but the list of writers who can command a meeting and get a purchase off a pitch are dwindling. There is no need for single-script anxiety, if you know where you're going and how to get there—AND have the discipline to execute a good concept. This text will draw you that map to show you what is important, how to stay focused, and how to complete your script in a timely fashion.

There are a few books I always have around to reference when I'm writing, cornerstones you may call them. Many of them go into detail about meta-character motivations, parallel dialog, inciting incidents, thesis and antithesis, etc.... This book stays focused on the story of your screenplay and how to achieve it in an efficient amount of time, while referencing some of these other works, writers, and educators. It also focuses on the mechanics of story like structure, plot movement and character functions. To give you a better sense of the art, it also gives context to the history of the craft and touches on adaptation. In addition to all of that, I'm going to do it while speaking to you like a normal person. Everything I write in this text is meant to assist you in removing obstacles to tell a great story that others will enjoy. Remember that stories are meant to edify and entertain. Your process is your process. Don't feel pressured, and write as quickly or slowly as you need to do good work. Writing good stories is not a race. Write well.

There are on average six hundred films produced each year in the United States, as well as nearly five hundred TV shows, and there are tens of thousands of solicited scripts, and many, many more unsolicited. Your chances of being produced are less than 1 percent. However, if you want to get your stuff read by the people that matter, then you need to be writing screenplays with good stories and solid structures, or your stuff will never see the light of day. This book will help you do that. Wallace Stegner, writing professor at Harvard, said that "talent can't be taught, but it can be awoken." I will attempt to wake you up. Screenwriting is largely a skill and you need to understand the foundational principles of structure and design. What I want you to be encouraged by is that screenwriting is a set of skills that can be learned. There are those out there that are just God-gifted writers, but for those of us who need to work our butts off, there is hope in practice.

Here are some things I want you to remember before you begin writing and after you finish:

1. You should be a student of writing forever. You never stop learning. Life and writing have that in common.
2. You must commit to the process of writing. Half-assed effort will get you half-assed pages.

3. Good writing takes practice. Write—a lot. Prepare to write more than one script. Don't get stuck with your *opus* script.
4. Your first screenplay might not be the next Oscar sleeper hit. Nothing wrong with hoping for luck, but don't hang your hat on it.
5. At some point you're going to fail. Failure is not bad, it teaches us. So fail quickly and fail forward in the proper direction.

These concepts are completely adaptable to your process. Find what works for you and go. If you fail, try it a different way. Failing forward is a superb way to learn. Just ask any scientist. The principles of screenwriting have been shared by many great writers and teachers. These principles are eternal (i.e. structure, Jungian archetypes, character arcs, plot maps, beat sheets, etc.). What I have done is compiled certain ideas from these many different ways of thinking and combined them in a way that best serves what I believe to be an efficient and structurally sound first draft—put simply. It is no-nonsense world building with complex elements that you have prepared. It will work in any genre for any style of film. I have placed exercises at the beginning of each chapter. Hopefully they will allow you deeper access into the concepts. Do them, don't cheat. The concepts are written for you to find a way in which you can understand and apply them authentically in your own writing.

Lastly, I want to encourage you. Writing is a historic art form of communication. What you do has value and you should be proud of your efforts. Some scripts will work and some will not, but following a dream to be a successful writer is not always a bad idea. Remember that you have value and worth as a writer, and without you the world would be a darker place. Writers shine the light in places many people choose not to look. Good luck and I truly hope this book helps you in every way.

CHAPTER 1

History of Screenwriting

We are so lucky as writers to be able to stand on the shoulders of giants. None of us have had to create from scratch the medium that we work in. All the rules have been canonized. While trends and expectations change, the basis for practical screenwriting has already been firmly cemented. It is now incumbent upon us to change things for the better, but that's not what this text is about. This text is about the writing and how great writing over time invented a form of storytelling. Hence, giants. The term perfectly allows us to visualize where we are and where we came from. I like the analogy like I like Ben Affleck. It's a guilty pleasure. I've heard all the criticisms of him: he's just another Hollywood cutie relying on charm and no acting chops, and he didn't really write *Good Will Hunting*. Well, I just don't care. I like to watch him work, well except in *Gigli*. And then came *Argo* and *The Town*. "TOLD YOU SO!" And he's a great Batman. Sorry, I digress. Let's begin by going back to the beginning, where the giants of screenwriting stood firmly on the ground, by themselves, before they were even referred to as screenwriters.

The advent of the Western drama began with Aristotle. Three principles of dramatic structure. Unity of time, unity of place, and unity of action. The last is the most specifically important to writers of visual media. Unity of action posits that there should be a story line that persists throughout the story and that any subplots should have their importance mitigated to the extent that the main through line is the most dominant. Aristotle wanted a main story to push the action and not get bogged down with competing, less important story lines. Journalists would call this burying the lead with less important headlines. Let's make this simple: characters make decisions and act on them, which makes the story move forward. This is the underpinning of all the movies and TV shows today. Characters that make decisions and ACT on those decisions. The decisions are the devices that push stories forward. It is one of the elements that we teachers harp on in screenwriting classes, which is to keep the story moving forward.

As the antiquated understanding of plays began to be reflective of a more complex society, playwrights developed characters with multifaceted backstories that directly affected character choices, and thereby affected their actions. A character who had been beaten by their father, even if this was only implied on the stage, makes a choice based on their experiences before the play takes place. The audience is invited into the intellectual process by being asked to infer certain things, and then to judge the character's action that takes place on the stage. This allowed plays to become more than what was happening on stage, but the result of what happened before. It meant that playwrights understood their characters as people and the play incorporated the sum of their experiences into their decisions. Complex characters allowed for more meaningful and relevant drama, and drama is what keeps us going back to the theater, the cinema, and our beloved televisions sets.

Dramatic writing was codified in Europe by William Archer in 1912, *Play-Making: A Manual of Craftmanship*, and then in the United States in 1919 by George Baker, *Dramatic Technique*. Silent films of the day borrowed from plays to formulate their scenarios into visually dramatic films. That's right, screenplays did not exist yet. Early films were not stories, but merely snapshots of life. A literal moving picture of a moment in time. What was once depicted in a still photo of a single moment, now could be presented over several moments. It was a huge leap forward in technology that opened a door to the future. A man sneezing, a train crash, a fire engine driving, scenarios that were action filled were the world's earliest films. These weren't stories as of yet, but it is interesting that they were pure action. This fascination with action is a pervasive element in a majority of storytelling forms.

Pictures, whether they were moving or not, would make it seem to be common sense that films should be visual, but it was not that simple. These films had to visually show drama, because even if there was sound, the largely immigrant population did not speak English. Situations had to be dramatic. The craft of visual storytelling erupted from this notion as much as the technological limitations of the day. That craft of telling stories visually continues today despite the ability for dialog. The old axiom a picture is worth a thousand words is very true.

The more technologically advanced things became, the more these early filmmakers could exploit it. For instance, unlike the play, film allowed for multiple story lines to be told in parallel. Two stories could be told out of sequence to build anxiety. One of the first instances of this can be seen in the 1902 film *The Life of an American Fireman*. This film shows the action of a fireman trying to get to a house that is on fire, while simultaneously telling the story of the woman inside. At this point in history writers and directors were often the same. They jotted down dramatic ideas on napkins and scraps of paper and went out to shoot them. It is ironic, but it is exactly what we tell writers and filmmakers not to do today.

The early 1900s gave way to writing accessible short scenarios. As the technology allowed for longer films, writers were needed to set up dramatic situations and maintain that tension for the length of the reel; however, films had a documentary feel to them. The longer the films got, the more a writer was needed. These early writers were blazing their own trail with no context. They were literally learning how to translate literary ideas (classic literature) dramatically, which was the norm at this time in history, into actionable moving pictures. To do this successfully, scenarios had to touch on common themes that were relatable to common people. The most popular of these was peril. Snidely Whiplash, a comedic carton version of a Victorian villain, tied his victims to train tracks. A hero would race in at the last moment and save the damsel in distress. This is a good way for you to relate to peril; however, know that this really only happened twice in the silent film era (*Eddy at the Throttle* and *Barney Oldfield's Race for Life* by Mack Sennet), and both films were comedies poking fun at the trope. Any silent film fan may lose their mind if you bring this up. Be warned. Just know that peril was a common theme and it allowed for the film version of ideal heroes to be born on screen.

Filmmaking was not sexy or admired at this time in history; in fact, they were looked down upon by the intellectuals of society. Actors had to provide their own wardrobe and travel, and were not paid very well. Locations were just accessible areas that scenarios could be shot for free or very little. For example, Gene Gauntier was a stage actress who began writing scenarios by the dozen. It was out of necessity really. The director began to run out of ideas and Gauntier stepped in. She was well read, and had a good understanding of literary design and the ebb and flow of dramatic writing. She was offered $20 per scenario. It is interesting that at the time directors were only paid $10 per film. This value dynamic would change, and directors would become the more valued asset. How could anyone write five to seven fulfilling scenarios (films) per week? Listen to Gauntier in her own words,

The woods were full of ideas. The surface had barely been scratched. A poem, a picture, short story, a scene from a current play, a headline in a newspaper. All was grist that came to my mill. There was no copyright law to protect authors and I could, and did, infringe upon everything.... I learned to dip into books, read a page almost at a glance, disentangle the plot in an hour, then lying face downward on the bed, compel my mind to shoot off into the byways, twisting and turning the idea until it was different as possible from the one that suggested it. Then to the typewriter to embroider the bare plot with the details of "business," scenic suggestions and original personalities. During the next three years I do not believe I read a book through for mere pleasure.

Borrowing and stealing from intellectual property, primary sources, and headlines is nothing new. This may be some of the earliest examples of adaptation. It is also interesting to see that writers had the majority of creative power in these early days. As I said, this trend has since completely reversed itself where writers are valued for content, but not in the process of making the film. As for Gauntier, she went on the write and star in *Hiawatha*, *The Scarlet Letter*, and the first filmed version of *Ben Hur*.

As we approach 1910, production companies realized the need for a constant stream of new content as people became bored quickly. Companies began to employ story departments to fill the need. Good scenario writers could expect to receive a decent salary, which was $40 per week at the time; however, this new design placed writers into a system where they became mere employees. Metaphorically, they became factory workers with little regard for the talent and skill necessary to create dramatic content out of thin air. The creative power that they once had began to erode rapidly. Incidentally, story editors (scenario writers) employed by film companies were mostly women at this point, which is another situation that dramatically shifts over time. Women at this time in history read literature, and therefore had a more firm concept of structure and character design. Their ability to churn out complex, fulfilling, and visual scenarios was unmatched. This would begin to change drastically as films entered into the age of sound and three-reel length. It also may be no coincidence that as power and money began to flow in earnest and men returned from World War I, women were drummed out of the business. It is an embarrassing truth, and it was accompanied by the prevalent thought that writers were not artists, but functionaries.

The three-reel movie is significant, as the technical process of changing reels became the rhythm to which current and modern films are still tapping. Screenwriters had to have increased skills at this point. Scenarios had to place a cliff hanger moment prior to a reel change to keep the audience engaged. This is where the five-act dramatic structure shifted to the three-act structure we are all used to today. This still exists today, and while some films may stray, the industry does not typically like structural change. The three-act structure, while breaking from traditional five-act plays, allows for more focused dissemination of information on the screen.

As we approach 1915, words began to become more and more relevant by invading the screen. Intertitles became pervasive and provided more than just transitions (*Next Day, Back Home at the Ranch*) and began to provide exposition. Anita Loos was a joke writer from New York City who ended up selling over one hundred stories to the film industry between 1912 and 1915. She became a highly sought-after intertitle writer for her ability to provide expository information in a short quippy form. As we fast forward toward the 1930s, women were for the most part out of the writing business in film due to the advent of sound in pictures. Women were thought to be too emotional to write strong male roles. Francis Marion was one of the only female survivors and managed to write two male-dominated machismo films that won Academy Awards: *The Champ* (1931) and *The Big House* (1932).

In the 1920s production companies began to look for very specific marketable elements in their films. Borrowing from the melodrama, with the ability to change in various ways, the following elements were standard for produced films:

1. An accessible protagonist with a relatable goal,
2. A clear antagonist who relentlessly opposes this goal,
3. An escalation of conflict in act II,
4. An act III climax in the form of confrontation, and
5. A fulfilling resolution.

This formula may feel very familiar as it is not far off from what production companies identify as marketable projects today. Think about the tent pole studio feature. It requires a relatable and likable protagonist, played by a bankable attachment. The film needs an antagonist who seems nearly unbeatable. The structure of the second half of act II is often where the bad guys seem to be at the point of victory. The good guy gets their stuff together and prepares for the final battle in act III. The ending must be amazing! Of course, some things have changed with additional requirements like the four-quadrant film, which touches multiple demographics, like the international market, teens, over forty, both men and women, etc. The calculus that goes into making features today is much more complex, but the basics remain very close to the same.

During this era journalists from New York flooded the Hollywood ranks; even though they considered it low-brow work, the money was too easy and too good to refuse. Journalists were perfectly matched to write for the films of this day. Their skill sets allowed them to write quality work while meeting deadlines. Some of these were Donald Ogden Stuart, Robert Benchley, Dorothy Parker, George S. Kaufman, and most notably Herman Mankiewicz and Ben Hecht. Mankiewicz even referred to the movies as "Slop, tripe, vomit." It did not stop him, however, or others in any way from writing for the money. Nor did it stop them from writing Oscar-worthy films. Hecht won the first Academy Award for writing with *Underworld* (1929) and Mankiewicz for *Citizen Kane* (1942). They understood the need for complex characters. Hecht went further by understanding how an audience could empathize with a villain, so he reached back into his Chicago reporting days and gave them a likable villain in Bull Weed. About Underworld he said,

> I made up a movie about a Chicago gunman and his moll called Feathers McCoy. As a newspaperman, I had learned that nice people ... the audience ... loved criminals, doted on reading about their love problems as well as their sadism.... The thing to do was to skip the heroes and heroines, to write a movie containing only villains and bawds. I would not have to tell any lies.

Classic authors of note were soon to join the ranks of reporters and journalists, which continued throughout the years. Some of these were F. Scott Fitzgerald, William Faulkner, Michael Chabon, Dave Eggers, Ray Bradbury, Aldous Huxley, and William Goldman.

In 1928, sound was in and actors had to talk on camera. This caused a major shift in the talent pool. It also dramatically changed writing, as now scenario writers were expected to write dialog. This is the moment that writers became known as screenwriters. This level of writing took on a new shape and a much higher level of skill. Dialog allowed writers to delve much deeper into characters and tell stories that had more than met the eye. Writers have had to adapt to technological advances since the advent of the film industry, and in this author's opinion, this is an indispensable part of the process. While there are many pieces to the moviemaking machine, there are no other pieces that create parts out of thin air, save for the screenwriter. *All great and terrible films begin on the page with the words FADE IN.*

You may wonder why history is even included in this book. It is because knowledge is power. It is important to be aware of the space a screenwriter inhabits in the filmmaking process and a historical reference point to accompany that understanding. Writers are incredibly adaptable and have been able to exploit technology, relevant news stories, great literary classics, and completely new content in which to tell great stories in a multitude of media. Dana Coen (*NCIS, JAG, Bones*) and I have discussed at length the importance of understanding the contribution of writers historically. It is a topic that is often not studied in relation to screenwriting. It is my contention that understanding the history of screenwriters actually makes you a better writer. While it is indirectly linked to writing itself, to be sure, I think it to be true.

There is much to this story, but what I find important is that no matter where we are in history it has been the writer that supplies the blank page with words so that a story can be told to an audience. It is the writer who is the catalyst to create great drama. Writers are indispensable and have great value. They adapt to financial change in film, as well as instantly incorporate technological advances. I encourage you to do a little research and see how hard many writers have fought for their rights. For instance, how writers had to adapt to the Hays Code, and the terrible time and sacrifice of the blacklisted writers. These men and women are the giants that I spoke about earlier, and we are in their debt for their most difficult trailblazing.

As you move forward in your career as a writer, I would like to leave you with some personal pleas that seem to have been supported by history. First, know that as writers we have value. That writers often shine lights in dark places where most others are afraid to even look. Writers can inspire technology and social evolution. Those who learn to write know how to communicate and can be the voice for those who do not have one. Last, writers create stories that can teach empathy. While this choice of job can be lonely and without success for long periods of time, it is incredibly important and has immeasurable value.

I think that about covers it. It should give you a little perspective into the history of this craft and art form. Now we can move on to writing your big idea.

CHAPTER 2

Weeks 1–2: Story, Plot, and Premise

Exercise: Without looking up the definition, write in one sentence the premise to your story. Don't worry about getting it wrong, just write it down. Take a few minutes and do it now. Remember just one sentence. Keep your premise close by as you read the chapter.

Before you write word one, you should understand at least three things. What is story, plot, and premise? First, you must have a premise—an idea. The premise is usually in the form of a "what if" question. My friend David Mickey Evans, writer and director of *The Sandlot* and *Radio Flyer*, said to one of my classes that "this is the most powerful question any writer can ask." It goes something like this: "What if a penniless artist wins a ticket on the greatest ship ever built?" or, "What if an over-the-hill science teacher gets a shot at the major leagues?" or, "What if a beloved general becomes a slave?" Your story will develop out of the answer. And the answer may be another question. Either way the premise is the catalyst for your story to grow. It is the instrument you will use to explore the story and how it will ultimately end satisfactorily. A good premise will always keep you reaching into the heart of the story, even when you are in the middle of the second act and contemplating seppuku. A premise must accompany a story, even if you know the story first. In other words, if you come up with a story first, find the premise ASAP, because it reveals why a protagonist will be so determined to achieve their goal. Lock in a premise and it will shed light on your story and allow you to go deeper.

Story is the main thing and you need to keep the main thing the main thing. Story is what the film is about, NOT what happens. What is the story of Ridley Scott's *Gladiator*? It's not what you think. This film is about a father and husband getting revenge for the death of his family. That is the story. Lots of things happen, but they are not the story. In my experience writers usually blow it by stumbling right out of the gate and not understanding their story.

Here is a scenario that may be familiar to you. A student writer comes to a professor with an idea. Awesome!

> Professor: Tell me what your story is about.
>
> Student: A heavyweight contender hurts himself before a title fight, so the champ chooses a loser with no chance at winning to take his place, but the loser is determined and takes the champ all the way to the eleventh round.
>
> Professor: Wow! What a great plot. So, what's the story?
>
> Student: Huh? That is the story.
>
> Professor: In that case it sucks.

The student posts their emotional pain on their Twitter or Instagram feed, and then the professor gets called into the dean's office. All this could have been avoided! The problem with the preceding idea was that there was *no* story and *all* plot. Story is big, macro, the entire enchilada, not the little details. Think of it this way. Plot is design. It is the line on a map from departure to arrival. The map itself is story, so the plot exists within the story. Premise is the idea that made you get the map out. Let's try using a piece of clothing as a metaphor. A sweater.

WHAT IF WE WERE TO KNIT A WARM GARMENT OUT OF
    YARN? = PREMISE.
SWEATER = STORY
YARN = PLOT

An idea is nothing without action. A ball of yarn is not a sweater, and a sweater does not exist without yarn, and neither exists without an idea. You need all three to develop a good film.

The plot is the sequence of events that pushes the story to completion. It is the design where the story is formed. If we stay with the film *Gladiator*, we follow Maximus as he falls from being a general to a slave and his rise from slavery to facing the Emperor of Rome. Plot is active, it moves the story through choices and actions. When we break *Gladiator* down, we get the following (*spoilers ahead*):

> Premise: What if a general becomes a slave?
>
> Story: A former Roman general seeks to avenge the death of his family by killing the emperor.

Plot: A widely loved Roman general is set to be executed by the new young emperor, who promises to kill his family and set an example for obedience. The general escapes, however, only to find his family murdered. Nearly succumbing to his injuries he is taken as a slave and finds himself in backwater gladiator arenas where he distinguishes himself quickly. His reputation brings him to Rome itself where he has an opportunity to face off with the young emperor on the sands of the Colosseum.

Now let's get back to our student with the boxing idea. A good professor would have advised them on the following. Start with a premise and ask yourself this: *What if* a run-down boxer had the opportunity to fight for the heavyweight championship of the world? Now that your potential story is framed in a solid premise, we can start working.

Premise: What if a run-down boxer had the opportunity to fight for the heavyweight championship of the world?

Story: An underdog boxer finds love and self-worth by fighting the heavyweight champion of the world.

Plot: The heavyweight champion of the world needs a replacement fighter because of an injury to a contender. To increase his record, he chooses a down-on-his-luck boxer and is stunned by his determination when the fight goes all the way to the eleventh round.

A good professor would also congratulate the student on writing *Rocky*.

This isn't a gimmick. It is the absolute fundamental beginning and foundation of every screenplay. If you don't know each one of these three things, then you don't have a solid enough understanding of your idea, and any time writing at this point beyond notes, sketches, and outlining would be a complete and total waste of time. I understand the temptation to put pen to paper, but you can't write what you don't know.

Premise is that question that consistently forces a writer to deliver on an idea. Story is what your screenplay is about, and plot is how it gets there. "Story is a metaphor for life encompassing real people doing real things, tender, malicious, evil, benevolent etc." (Robert McKee, *Story: Substance, Structure, Style, and the Principles of Screenwriting*). Plot is the means by which we as an audience can navigate through a story. Good story trumps good plot. No story—no film! Watch any Martin Scorsese film and watch him command story. Remember that story cannot be told without exceptional characters.

More on that later. Let's look at the original canon of dramatic work written by Aristotle himself.

Aristotle's Dramatic Elements:

Plot
Character
Theme
Dialog
Music
Spectacle (event or change)

The sum of all these is what we modern writers refer to and define as STORY. Let's break it down into simple statements. Premise is the QUESTION that keeps us probing through the heart of the story. Plot is what HAPPENS, and story is what the movie is ABOUT. Being able to identify the differences will prove to be an important factor in your writing, directing, or producing.

Robert McKee says, "And as in all things political, the distortion of the truth is greatest at the extremes." What I took away from this is that whatever the circumstances you choose for your plot, they should be extreme or put your characters in extreme positions. Your characters need to be put under tremendous strain by the plot, to reveal who they truly are. These extreme situations, resulting in choices, push the plot forward or we would have mostly boring movies. Think about this in the *Rocky* premise. A boxer who has no business getting an opportunity to fight for the championship gets a shot. That is extreme. The character's personal circumstances are extreme (poverty), and therefore it makes for great drama. Time for another ridiculous metaphor, a road trip. Try it this way:

Premise: What if two handicapped guys were to take a road trip?

Story: Two lonely handicapped men find friendship and confidence while on a cross-country road trip.

Plot: Two grumpy and lonely men, one deaf man and one blind, escape from a hospital and take a road trip across the country in a convertible Mustang, and find that they are not as helpless as they thought.

We have the question that keeps pushing us forward. We have a story, and we have a way to navigate through the story with extreme characters under tremendous pressure. Now that is a movie. I wonder if you recognize it?

Symmetry of Opposites

The symmetry of opposites is an idea I came to after reading and writing a lot of scripts. The good ones had it and the bad ones didn't. A lot of my philosophy in writing hovers around balance. As we develop the stories in our minds, we often find that what a protagonist wants is not what they find, but it is what that character needs, and therefore the ending is satisfying. I use the term want and need often to describe this pull in two directions by characters. The yin and yang of life is not so different, and I think that fiction needs to reflect life for it to be accessible. Having said that, it also needs to be exceptional. Later on, I will discuss the symmetry of opposites in character functions, and story beats that have opposing movement, but I also like the idea of poetic balance. This means that our lead character gets what they need, but they have to pay for it. For instance, in *Hunger Games*, Katniss is a righteous character opposed to oppression and murder, but she *must* kill to win. The killing takes something from her, even though she may be successful in the end. The reason the ideas of light versus the dark, good versus evil, pleasure versus pain are so appealing, is because we can relate and ascribe values to them. The idea of the symmetry of opposites is more nuanced than winning or losing. This is more like winning but regretting what you lost to win. A few examples are in the film *The Hollars* (Jim Strouse) where the symmetry of opposites is a birth and a death, the joy and the grief. In *The Wrestler* (Robert Siegal), it is hope and disappointment. In *Warrior* (Anthony Tambakis), it is a victory and a defeat. Each one of these meets a poetic balance that satisfies us, but also creates a real-world–style conflict that allows us access to a story in a personal way. That emotional access provides us with something to attach to. That attachment piece is more specifically defined as a theme. Which quite cleverly leads me to the next section.

Theme

Theme is something that I find most students and screenwriters leave out completely. Theme is that thing that follows us out of the theater and sticks with us for a while. It is a question of perspective for the main character, for the audience, and from the author. It is the lesson that is learned. It is the moral compromise that the protagonist is placed under. For example, a character may say that "things aren't always as they seem." True enough, but how does this affect you in the seat, and how does your protagonist learn something from this? When I write theme, I usually want to send the audience home with something. I know that most of us don't deal with ex-KGB agents or off-the-grid operatives, but even they can learn the lesson, "Things aren't always what they seem," and perhaps that is what we go home with. At the very least it is another layer of entertainment that rings very close to the real world. Theme allows us to make connections to our own lives in a relevant way. It is something of value accessible by the audience that they can extract out of the fantasy of film to take home with them. Think about the Charlie Brown holiday shows and how we all went away learning something about ourselves at Charlie Brown's expense. No matter the genre it works. For instance, *American Beauty* and *Office Space*. Both films, although different genres and budgets, have great themes. If you screen both movies you will hear it somewhere in the first act. These two movies collectively ask, "What would happen if we ceased to cling to social expectations (society's demands of the rat race), and should we do what makes us happy instead of meeting collective social expectations?" This idea allows us access to a personal question within us all, and therefore makes the story experience deeper and more fulfilling.

In most good films some character will state it, usually directly to the protagonist. It may go by as an innocuous bit of dialog, but it sits in our mind, in our subconscious, and allows us to ponder. I believe it to be an inseparable part of story, and when I read a script without one, it leaves a hole for me. Theme adds a third dimension to story and a target for plot. It is so important to me, in fact, that it is one of the things I decide on before I write the first word. Sometimes when I'm writing, the theme changes and I find a deeper one, but the idea is always there pushing me to have the characters striving to learn something, fail at something, and teach us something. Theme improves a story as much as perspective did for painting in the Renaissance.

Let's review what is important:

Premise: The question that helps us frame our story. It is most useful in the form of a *"what if"* question.

Story: It is the answer to the premise and what the film is *about*. It's that one sentence that encapsulates everything broadly.

Plot: This is what *happens* in the film, and it pushes the story forward. Remember that plot is a series of events strung together. It must be active,

Theme: This is the eternal question. It is the interactive part of the script, allowing readers access to the story through a shared *lesson* or *experience*. It's the piece the audience should leave with by asking themselves how they compare. You must know these things and have them squarely in your mind *before* you write word number one.

Exercise: Try writing the premise, story, plot, and theme to the following two movies.

Sling Blade	*The Godfather*
Premise: _____	Premise: _____
Story: _____	Story: _____
Plot: _____	Plot: _____
Theme: _____	Theme: _____

CHAPTER 3

Weeks 3–4: Organizing Creativity

Exercise: Look back on the premise you wrote down at the beginning of the previous chapter. How would you change it? Rewrite it now suggesting a determined protagonist. Use that to write a one-sentence logline (story), three sentences of plot (acts 1–3), and one sentence for theme. Don't worry about getting it wrong. The exercise helps get your mind in the right place. Keep these close, as we will use them later.

If you are anything like me, and like many writers I know, you just want to write. Paper, pen, laptop, and for those that still write in the '70s, typewriter. Let's go man, I've got it! Hold the frickin' phone. Now is the time you have to become acquainted with your story. Believe me, whatever you have can get a whole lot better with a little bit of time.

Some of my writing colleagues may be laughing their butts off at that last statement, because of my, let's say speedy nature. Friend and writing partner Vince McKewin (*The Replacements, Fly Away Home, Las Vegas*) calls it A. T. time—*Acosta Time*. This is the rapid amount of time I spend on turning a draft around. It is true that I spit out drafts quickly, but I'm prepared. I spend the time thinking things through way ahead of time. I have the premise, the story, the plot, the theme in my head. I also attempt to inhabit my characters to understand them more fully. So, quick is not always best by *any* measure. Best is best. Some work differently, and fast or slow doesn't indicate a good or bad writer. For me, however, I do the intellectual work, which allows me to do the writing quickly. Going off half-cocked is stupid, whether fast or slow. Take that from me. I've tried both.

Here's an example:
INT. Smoky Bar – Night
STUDENT (20s) looks across the room and spots her. SHE (20s) has got the look and she knows it. They are strangers, but this night is magical. Student wastes no time and slides onto the well-used bar stool next to her.

STUDENT

You've got it goin' on, little girl.

SHE

I know. Ain't so bad yourself.

Student throws his shot glass back and wipes his mouth with his flannel sleeve.

STUDENT

Let's get married.

She throws her arms around him in a loving embrace. Their matching flannel fabrics spark with static electricity.

SHE

How could I say no?

FADE OUT.

How ridiculous is that? Pretty far-fetched and sinfully cliché. However, what is the difference between that scene and having an idea and going straight to script? It is just as ridiculous, I assure you. You need time to ruminate, meditate, and other types of *-tates* to get to know your story. Is your story the result of the premise? What is the plot and how will it serve the story? Your characters become very important here. Most likely you already have a lead character (protagonist) in mind, and probably a B character as well, but what about everyone else? Who are they? What are their names? Are their names indicative of who they are, or is this not that type of movie? Overall, this is the time that you really flesh out all of your ideas and make them become a part of your own DNA. I am a proponent of discovery. I believe that you will explore, experiment, and discover during the writing process; however, explorers don't go on adventures without being prepared. They almost always start with a map, sextant, compass, and other Middle Age instruments of exploration. You should too. It is time to organize your creative muscles.

The story as you begin to understand it at this point may change. It *will* change as a matter of fact, but that doesn't mean you can't understand it. Syd Field famously says, "If you don't know, who does?" How true. You really have to know what happened, what is happening, and what will happen. You must be sure of all of this before you start writing. I've gone off half-cocked many times in my career, and it always ends up in a major rewrite or a strongly worded e-mail from a writing partner/producer expressing large doses of exasperation. Or a simple f**k you. Depends on the day.

After you have really thought deeply about your story and WRITTEN out the *premise, story,* and *plot,* begin to share. I know many people out there have scared you to death with the threat of someone stealing your story. Well, I'm sure it has happened before, but not a huge risk in my opinion. Good scripts are all about execution and practice. So tell your story to everyone you know. What are their reactions? Is it a cool idea? Is it interesting? Do any of them even give a crap? Funny thing is that when you start telling your story out loud, you will develop more ideas, better ideas, and your story and plot will be affected in a positive way. This is the time you allow yourself to be completely creative before the flurry of writing. This is where your imagination really runs the show. Every new idea should be jotted down somewhere, no matter how crazy. There are no wrong answers at this point.

Let me walk it back just a bit. If you are in LA, maybe don't tell your story to EVERYBODY. Be careful of the sleazy producer or the desperate writer, or the ... you get the point. Use good judgment; but you need to tell your story and see how it affects people. Having a safe place and community of story-tellers is a good idea. A place you can go to share and receive support and get ideas from like-minded people. Writing groups are a great place to get and give notes. Giving good notes are as important as receiving them. Friend and colleague Bobby Bowman (*My Name is Earl, Family Guy, It's Always Sunny in Philadelphia*) advocates for joining these groups not merely as a place to help your writing, but also as a place to get your career started. Never underestimate relationships and networking.

You need time to elaborate and develop. Stories began as an oral tradition, and there is a something very natural about telling stories. You will be amazed at what you can flesh out by speaking your story out loud and answering the questions that your listeners ask. Once you get people saying, "I want to see this movie," you know you're ready to go to paper.

A question one of my development partners, Brandon Jones (CAA, Morgan Creek), used to ask is, "Who cares?" In other words, he wanted to know if anyone would even care about your story. Is it about a pet owner who is trying to raise funds to get his dog fixed? Who cares? Someone must, or the film is a flop from the get. Remember who your market is. It is not the audience, it's the studios and production companies. These people want to see a concept that is cinematic. An idea that MUST be a movie. Terrio Rossio says, "The most important thing is whether the concept of the movie is intrinsically compelling. I like to feel with absolute certainty that the fundamental idea for a film is, without a doubt, an exceptional premise, You want to cross the finish line at the beginning of the race." Incidentally his script *Déjà Vu*, cowritten by Bill Marsilii, sold for $5.6 million.

How much time does it take to figure this out? I have no clue. There are no hard and fast rules. If you are in a class, your professor will most likely provide you with a finite amount of time, which is appropriate, but in the industry, this takes as much time as it takes. Spec scripts don't have deadlines to start. Begin when you're ready. If you're never ready to write, perhaps the story sucks or maybe you should rethink your career choice. You have to be the judge.

Some of the things in my process may help or you may have your own. If you don't have a process, try these on and see. Start by asking yourself some questions.

Do you know your character? You really need to know them, how they would react in certain situations. You can even put your character in a situation that they will never face in your script, but how do you think they would react based on how well you know them? This brings you closer to them and their motivations.

How well do you know the rules of the universe that you have created? Remember you are the god of this world, and your rules, while they may be fantastic, are still your rules. You and your characters should abide by them. Do they learn anything (theme)? You need to be prepared for the consequences of behavior change because of the lessons your characters learn, and therefore a change in action (plot) that visually shows a learned lesson. Fill up scrap pieces of paper, envelopes, notebooks, what have you. Be as creative as you can and then it's time to organize it into something you can use.

Preparation

I know that you have all heard the phrase prewriting. I also know that most of you hate and/or believe it to be a waste of time. I challenge that by saying that prewriting will save at least 25 percent of the total project time. At this point you have a premise that has turned into a story, and you have developed a plot to push the story forward, and a theme to allow the reader access to internal motivations. Then you took a time out and thought it through, developed characters etc. Now it is time to write it down. Guess what? Sometimes your imagination writes a check your laptop can't cash. Now is the time you have to figure out how to execute all your amazing ideas.

Start by writing a summary. I like to think of this as I would a dust jacket blurb. When you go to the book store and buy a book, you read a blurb on the back. It's like a novel trailer. That's what you should do now. Don't worry about grammar, spelling, neatness, or format. None of that matters. No one will ever see this. Some people call this writing a treatment. I think that a treatment is a lot more formal and it is meant as a readable document. What I am proposing here is to write whatever the heck you want. Cross things out, scribble, draw stick figures. Who cares? The only one that needs to understand what you are writing is you.

Vince McKewin and I were working on adapting my book, *The Virus Chronicles: The Culling,* into a TV series. After knocking ideas around for a month or so, he kicked out what he likes to call "the document." It is both general and specific, identifying beats, act breaks, and all sort of important and pointless crap. It had things we were unsure about, as well as necessary exposition. We could write anything we wanted, because no else sees this document except for us. It gave us a place to dump ideas or cut them. It was a safe place to mess things up and fix them, and when we were done, we had a solid beat sheet that allowed us to write and stay focused. No matter how far afield we wanted to go, the document forced us to stay anchored.

Having a safe document is the place that you need to become more specific. No more generalities. If you don't have some answers, now is the time to ask the tough questions. Who are your characters? You really need to give them names by now. You may have from one to eight main characters, but what about others? Secondary characters. You should have a good understanding of their personalities by now and how that directly affects the plot. All characters should have functions. *We'll get to that later.* Think about characters as real people. What are their motivations, flaws, desires, weaknesses?

You will run across problems here. Some of your twists and turns will intersect with the reality of the world you have created. Some of the scenes might ring far too convenient. For instance, a counter-terrorism expert is stuck in the middle of a terrorist attack. Well good thing for us, because he also knows how to rewire his cell phone to break into the FBI's radio channel. How convenient. Try this:

INT. JAIL CELL – NIGHT

Two men, MAN 1 & MAN 2 (40s), sit staring at a the heavily barred cell door. They are merely forgotten criminals with no hope.

MAN 1

If we only had a hack saw.

MAN 2

Yeah ... wait a minute.

Man 2 reaches under his mattress and pulls out a hack saw. First surprise, and then joy begins to glow within him.

MAN 2

My goodness. The guys who escaped before
we came in must have left this by mistake.

MAN 1

Wow. We really caught a break.

FADE OUT.

Wow indeed. Bobby Bowman (*Sprung*) gave me a great piece of advice: "If there is a coincidence it can hurt the protagonist, but not help them." Invariably you will have this moment in your script and it will need to be fixed. The time to fix it is when you have a page or two of text, not when you are sixty-eight pages in. Remember that a script is like a lake, if you drop even the smallest stone into the water it will create many ripples. Every time you change something in your script, it affects something else. I would rather rewrite two pages than fifty. This seems like common sense, but it took my development partner to teach it to me. Brandon Jones, a development exec at Morgan Creek, and I would spend hours on the phone working on scripts. He would say something needed changing, and I would say, but then I have to go back to act I and change all of that. He would answer by saying I should have thought about that when I wrote it the first time. Well *eff*-me!

Work out the problems, do the work, get frustrated, angry, whatever it is that you do. However, when you are done, and all the dust settles, you will be left with a strong summary and you understand your story even better.

Treatment and Outline

Now that the summary is done, you can concentrate on a formal document, one that is suitable to go out as a synopsis, treatment, or outline. What is a treatment? This is actually a question that has no definitive answer. Traditionally, the treatment is a document that spans anywhere from five pages to fifty. It contains a logline, character introductions, and a condensed version of your story highlighting the important beats. It has often been used in pitches to sell, as well as get talent attached. Recently these documents have taken on a different life. It may be surprising to you, but in Hollywood no one likes to read. That's right, in an industry predicated on a written script, no one likes to take the time to read them. Therefore, any version of a script that is in a condensed form, but highlights beats that are cinematic, helps sell it. It may also be used in production as a guide for those who are on the production team that have not read the script—yes, people who work on the film may never read the script either.

Do you need to write a treatment? No, you do not. However, from a writer's perspective, a treatment is good way to formalize your story into a visual example with the proper placement of plot points. A treatment does not need dialog. Can you have it? I suppose, but it is not necessary as this is a narrative. This document is expository. You are telling the story directly. All your creative ideas are now going into a formal setting.

Personally, I do not like treatments. I have written them, and they have been requested from me. I prefer outlines or beat sheets. These are shorter documents that use bullet points to designate actions and plot points specifically; however, this means I have to create another document that deals specifically with character as the outline doesn't cover that. Outlines work better for me, but as I said in the beginning, this isn't about a specific way to write, but how it works best for you. No matter which you choose, treatment or outline (or both), the idea is to be prepared before you write the first word. You need the questions answered, that is all. Figure out what form of preparation best gets your mind around the world you are building. In an academic setting there will be time restrictions, but in the world of spec writing, there are not.

Exercise: Collect all your notes, scribbles, doodles, and the premise, plot, and logline from earlier. Rewrite your summary into a more organized summary/ treatment with all the necessary changes, but don't throw away your old stuff. You never know if you might need it again. When you are done you should read it out loud to yourself. It may be one page or twenty pages long. Doesn't matter, whatever works for you.

Question: Does it read like a cogent story. Is it engaging? Do you (or anyone who reads this) want to know more? Does it sound like a movie? If yes, you are now prepared to really get down to work. Have a copy standing by as you move on to the next chapter. If no, back to the drawing board and do it again. It's time well spent.

CHAPTER 4

Weeks 5–6: A Study of Structure in Three Acts

Exercise: Write down the four most important parts of your story that you should know *before* writing. Don't look it up, just answer what you believe to be true. Each part should be no more than one sentence long.

There are many ways to skin a cat. I say this, but I have to admit that I have never skinned a cat. I don't think I would skin a cat, and to be honest I have no idea why the hell anyone would want to skin a cat. I mean, they are arrogant little bastards, but they hardly deserve skinning. Unless your cat happens to be the black cat in a Rod Serling episode that smothers a kid or something. Other than that, I have no idea why cats get such a bad rap. Let's get down to the business of structure.

There is no one way to process the approach to structure. The operative word being process. There is very little difference, if any, in actual structure once a work is written. There are many different ways to approach structure. This is called paradigm, and it has been argued and written to death. The thing is that a structure is only as strong as the characters who travel it. There must be a motivating factor that keeps them moving forward, and the popular term for this is through line. Okay, here's another metaphor. I want you to imagine a tin can telephone. For those of you too young to remember, this is when you attach a string to a pair of tin cans and you pretend to hear one another. No, you can't text on a tin can phone, geez! So, if you take away the string you have only a couple of cans that don't connect. Get it? Probably not. The through line connects the beginning and the end of a story just like the string connects the cans. Disconnect the string and you only have two cans, not a pretend phone. Disconnect a through line in a story and you only have a bunch of scenes thrown together that are not held in place and do not tell a cogent or engaging story. Let's take the film *Killing Them Softly* (Andrew Dominik). This is an adaptation from a George Higgins novel. Let's focus on finding the through line. Let me help, you can't. The script meanders from an illegal high-stakes card game robbery, set up by the owner to hit himself, and moves into a series of mob killings by rival mob bosses and hired assassin(s). Then there is the attempt to link politics and crime as a metaphor and a corporate-style CEO as a mob boss, human greed, and self-loathing, survival … let me stop here. Gandolfini and Pitt are great. They are always great, but it is their performance that makes them so, not the material. The photography is equally as good. It's gritty, super noir, and really well composed, but the point is that the through lines are ambiguous and don't connect the beginning to the end. Honestly, the script was just not good, and Dominik attempted to put too much in. He failed to identify what was important and dramatic, which is not uncommon in adaptation—at least in my opinion. We'll discuss adaptation specifically in a later chapter. The shooting was good, the noir elements good, but style can't make up for a bad script. You should check out *The Assassination of Jesse James by the Coward Robert Ford, written and directed by Dominik, which was well written and shot.*

Let's try another film and one that is a guilty pleasure for me, *Signs* (M. Night Shyamalan). I like this movie, but I think that I like it because of how powerful the cast is. Mel Gibson and Joaquin Phoenix are exemplary and pull the story through with their performances. Rory Culkin and Abigail Breslin really allow the audience to access them at an emotional level. That said, it has story issues and you should be warned as there are many *spoilers* ahead. There are two through lines, which by themselves are okay, but in this case they compete with one another. Through line one is about aliens who have mastered the science of intergalactic travel (which would be a race of beings that is ahead of Earth by approximately one hundred thousand years), and two the supernatural aspects of God actively participating in human lives (divine intervention). Through line one is a strong story. Aliens come to Earth to harvest … well something. Doesn't matter, they are the bad guys and we must fight them. Their visits to the planet leave SIGNS in corn fields. The second through line is interesting and mysterious, where God has chosen to affect the lives of a minister who has lost his faith and allowed his dead wife to tell the future by way of out-of-context SIGNS. Again, pretty interesting. The problem is that God and aliens don't mix in this case. Is our God their God? Since God is real, which God is He, and does this exclude all of the other religions? You see, there are far too many issues by mixing these two through lines. If you take out the supernatural aspect, in my opinion the movie still works without the confusing SIGNS. I know Shya-malan was probably positing that the signs may or may not have been real and that we choose to see them, but half of the story has the signs as actually real. I won't even bring up the fact that aliens who have developed a light speed drive can't figure out how to use a doorknob or identify that water (a toxin to them) covered over two-thirds of the planet. There is always a magic bullet the audience has to swallow, but more than one poses problems. As I said, I like the movie; it is very entertaining to me. I watch it every couple of years, but not because of the story.

There is some consensus in how many through lines there are in a story. Two for most features, although there are some that say four. Sometimes three in a TV series depending on if it's network or cable. The point is that there should be a main through line that connects the beginning to the end and all other through lines should be subordinate and not compete with the main story. Subplots are there to assist the story and help develop character.

There have been many paradigms and structure designs published by amazing writers and teachers, and they can get confusing, especially when you are told that THIS is the way. Well it ain't. All the structure paradigms that you have been taught and shown will have commonalities but use widely different vernacular. In essence, they are the same at the core. Some are more complicated, some are specific, some are character driven, some approach from an audience perspective or author perspective, but all have the same purpose of having you the writer arrive at the same place—a fulfilling ending. I'm going to break down the paradigms of some truly great writers and teachers, so that you don't have to. If any of these approaches tickle your fancy, you should probably pick up one of their books as well.

Michael Hauge, who is a lecturer and script consultant for Hollywood, believes in two through lines and that there are five requirements for the outer motivation (through line one) of a protagonist. These must be visible and apparent to the audience. The second through line is of the protagonist's inner journey, which must be dealt with prior to the film's end. Both through lines are attached to desire and unavoidable conflict. Hauge looks for meaning and therefore approaches the story from the author's perspective.

Robert McKee, one of the most famous teachers of Story on Earth, sees two through lines through one central plot. These are called the quest. One is the quest for their conscious desire, and the other is the quest for their unconscious desire. He approaches the story through the audience's perspective.

Chris Huntley describes four through lines due to what he believes is the brain's ability to see things from three direct perspectives and one indirect perspective. Providing an audience with all four through lines, which he describes as the grand argument, is ultimately satisfying. Linda Seger and Chris Vogler also have some interesting paradigms in which to approach structure.

The thing is that all these theories and through lines make me see double. After I study them, I just don't feel like writing. I feel like drinking, which is probably bias on my part, because I enjoy drinking. That is beside the point, however. I wanted something simple, but effective. How to get all that stuff into an easy-to-understand paradigm?

First, I like the idea of only two things to think about, and I believe the audience will too. Academics may call this the inner and outer journey. I call it *want* and *need*. What does a main character want and what do they need? I don't make a distinction between main character, hero, or protagonist. I even use the term lead sometimes. So very blue collar of me, I'm sure. I don't approach the paradigm through the perspective of audience or author, but from my character(s). They are facing the conflicts ahead, so I inhabit them and embrace their flaws. As the main character, I may know what I want, but perhaps don't know what I need, and therefore I go on my journey with an unreliable desire. This does not differ from McKee or Hague, except that I allow the story to unfold around me as a character instead of looking for meaning from another perspective. I think this makes for good story and great conflict, both internal and external, while demonstrating an authentic character.

To summarize, the main character has a want and a need. They accept a challenge and face conflict relentlessly moving toward what they want, but they must resolve the conflict of need as well. You can feel free to have any character you choose to tell this story, but as a writer you should be able to inhabit your character(s) and understand what it is like to be them. This will allow you to exploit their flaws in realistic fashion and as the god of your world have them succeed or fail at overcoming obstacles. How can we take this and apply it to structure?

I have chosen three ways that I find the most simple, concrete, and easy to execute. I will break them down and you get to experiment on which paradigm (or a combination) works best for the way you understand and write. That's right, I'm not telling you that my way is the way or that their way is the way. As long as you know what you are doing structure wise, understand the basics of structural paradigm, and the process works for you, that is all that counts. The adherence to structure, however, will be the basis for a good story told well. I want you to feel free to break the rules in all the ways that you can, but I also want you to be sure that you know exactly which rules you are breaking before you break them. The ignorant often claim that creativity and art drive the form and that prescriptive methods stop creative genius. That is pure hogwash. Yes, I used the term hogwash. No, I don't know exactly what hogwash is. I assume it is a detergent for cleaning swine. I am not quite sure why something like that would exist.

Structure is the hook that you hang the entire story on. It must be executed with a plan. Don't believe me? How about William Goldman (*Butch Cassidy and the Sundance Kid, Misery, The Princess Bride*) who said, "Screenplays are structure." Eloquent in its brevity, wouldn't you say? There is no producible story without a well-structured screenplay. If you don't agree, write all you want and decorate your walls with unproduced scripts.

Creative Methodologies

There are two broad creative methodologies to writing: deductive and inductive. There are scores of authors who are successful on both sides of the aisle. Inductive writing is the creative journey in which you write scenes not connected to a specific idea, but loosely correlated. By not being anchored down by a specific idea, your imagination is in control, allowing for amazing concepts to come through. After this journey of creativity, you collect all the ideas and put them together like a puzzle to begin to build a story or design a structure around the ideas if you will. I've done this with poetry and short stories. Quite honestly, I have come up with some amazing ideas this way, but they have never really amounted to anything more than a few scenes strung together. I have never been able to make a full-length story out of this process. It has helped improve projects that I already have structured, but I can't remember once where it became a story unto itself. This doesn't mean you can't. I prefer to use inductive writing merely as a brainstorming exercise or a way to catalyze a story. In other words, I try to flesh out ideas this way—big vision stuff. I use it in the preparation part of my personal method. I let my imagination, which is not restricted by any means, do the heavy lifting. Those ideas have to be pinned to a specific structure in my writing world.

Deductive writing is when you specifically outline your story or identify beats, placing scenes in specific places to move a story forward coherently. I prefer this method of writing and believe that for screenwriting it is a more appropriate way to be a professional success. I also think this makes better screenwriters. Critics will say that writing with a pure method is formulaic and lacks creativity. I say that a well-structured screenplay takes immense amounts of creativity to make new things happen within a commonly used literary infrastructure.

As a writer I find that structure is imperative. I harp on it in class, especially during a first draft. A good story told poorly but well-structured can be re-written and made into something exceptional by developing out characters, punching up dialog, increasing the stakes, etc. If the structure is bad, then the script needs to be rebuilt from the bottom up and that is a heavy lift. Structure is the foundation of your story. If a foundation is bad, you have trouble. Even an average script reads well with a good structure, so it is a good place to start.

Structure Design

I believe that Syd Field is probably the most notable author when it comes to structure. Perhaps you have already read his book. It was my first screen-writing book. He preaches the three-act structure. His structure method is designed around a story line that has four elements: the beginning, the end, plot point one, and plot point two with two pinch points. Let's take a look at a graphic that displays how Field sees the structure of a screenplay.

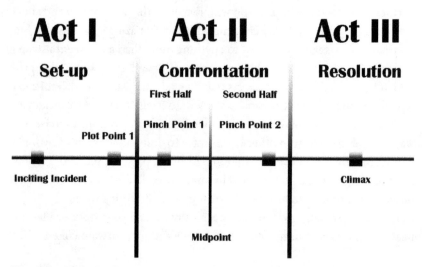

Fig. 1. Basic Three Act Structure

This is fairly simple, but deceptively so. Every structure method or process you learn, no matter how complex, is based off this paradigm. Field says that there are four things you must know *before* you start writing: the beginning, the ending, plot point one, and plot point two. I have tweaked this message in my teaching, but essentially it is the same. I usually use the road trip metaphor.

If you get in a car and go somewhere, how long will it take to get there? The answer is never, because you don't know where you are going. Or you might arrive at a dilapidated house filled with a satanic cult looking for a human sacrifice. Bad structure has consequences, people! You must know where you start and where you end. It creates the entire context of your story—the boundaries, if you will. Once you know these things, you need to identify what action will lead the protagonist into act II and what action will lead to act III. These four elements are the very foundation of the structure of your story. Field also indicates a midpoint, because the first half of the movie must be different from the second half. The world around the protagonist is changing, either internally or externally, but we need to see that—visually.

The steps will be, what is your starting point, and what does this side of the world look like? How will the protagonist deal with plot point one? In act II the protagonist begins to deal with this problem as they meet confrontation and they hit the midpoint. The world changes (second half), increasing confrontation. Now, how will the protagonist deal with plot point two in this new world? Finally the protagonist must solve the problem and come to a resolution, which lands us on the ending, which you should already know.

I teach that you need to know these four things, and no matter what structural design you use, these four things will find their way in. The problem I had after writing a screenplay—or five—was that while I had an immense amount of freedom to explore using this design, it also allowed me to stray too far afield. I needed less freedom as I tended to allow the inductive style of writing to influence me too much and couldn't seem to dial in on the story. For those of you who need the room to move, this is a great design to use.

The second way to identify structure is the sequence method. I believe many professors at New York University use this method. I also think it is a good deliverable for academic purposes. Sequencing is a way to further dial in on events that happen in each act. It is a little more complex, but it identifies necessary events that push the action of a story forward. There are eight sequences in a screenplay divided equally among the acts. Sequence one and two in act I, three through six in act II, and seven and eight in act III. At the end of each sequence there is a moment of choice and action that pushes it into the next sequence. Here's what a sequencing graph looks like.

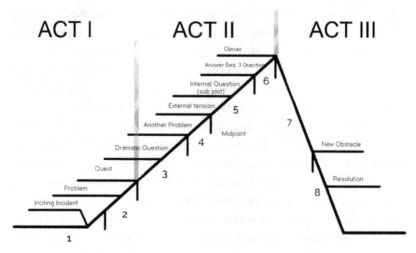

Fig. 2. Sequence Structure

As I said, each sequence represents a bit of action that pushes into the next sequence based on the choices of the protagonist. The design of the triangle shows us how the tension and release of the script should move. Let's identify the definition of each sequence.

Sequence 1 establishes the protagonist and contains the inciting incident. The inciting incident is the moment when the protagonist is faced with a choice that threatens to upend the world as they know it.

Sequence 2 provides the protagonist with the problem. They have accepted the challenge (inciting incident) and have moved forward, but then are faced with a problem. How will they proceed? This brings us into act II.

Sequence 3 is the quest of the protagonist. They have made their decision and try to fix the problems at hand. The tension is raised here, indicated by the triangle. This is where a dramatic question is posed for the protagonist to answer later.

Sequence 4 is where the protagonist is faced with more than they thought they were. Each solution is potentially faced with another problem, and the tension ratchets up. This leads us to the midpoint. The midpoint is the center of the movie and usually indicates a complete change in tone for the remaining part of the film.

Sequence 5 brings us into the part of the film where the protagonist is faced with problems both inside and out.

Sequence 6 is where the dramatic question of sequence 3 must be answered. The protagonist is at their lowest and something needs to change to allow them to go forward. The answer resolves second-act problems and the protagonist can now move forward with a plan, which leads us into act III.

Sequence 7 puts our protagonist square in the middle of the battle. The old problems are over and now there are new obstacles to get over.

Sequence 8 is resolution at last. The protagonist either wins or loses and faces the final tension. Resolution does not always mean the protag wins. Resolution is merely an ending to a problem.

By combining both structural designs we can see that there are commonalities. Let's take a look at how they stack up and compare. Field says act I is thirty pages of dramatic context with a specific beginning point that sets up the story and contains plot point one, which is a choice that creates an action on the part of the protagonist. Sequence 1 establishes the protagonist and inciting incident, which identifies a problem in sequence 2 that must be solved by the protagonist. The choice to do this pushes us into act II. The basic beats are the same, and when you overlay these two designs you will see similarities throughout.

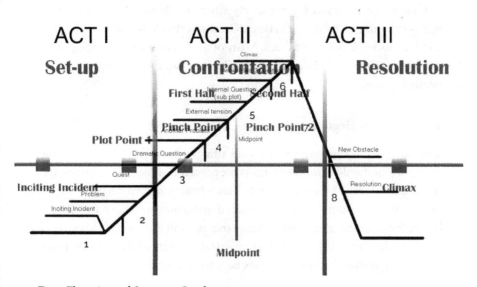

Fig. 3. Three Act and Sequence Overlay

Sequencing is useful by how it breaks up the prose into smaller parts, which may seem much less overwhelming to a writer. Having to turn out fifteen quality pages is much easier to concentrate on than one hundred pages or even thirty. The difficulty I run into is that the even nature of sequences seems to interrupt the natural rhythm of the story. In my screenplays, the idea of numerically even sequences is not something I could succeed at and therefore makes it difficult for me to use it as a structural writing template.

The final structural design I will discuss is beat writing. This is the design that I use in my own writing. In many ways it creates limitations, but what I find is that if I do the creative preparation beforehand, beat writing allows me to adhere to a proven producible model, while not sacrificing my story or limiting my creativity. It allows me to feel the rhythm of the writing hitting all major beats and plot points that the protagonist must act on to move the story forward. The two guys that come to mind who use this style are John Truby and the late Blake Snyder. Truby uses twenty-two "building blocks" to maximize tension and action. Snyder uses fifteen beats for the same reason. I tend more toward the Snyder method, but do not feel that exact page placement is the key. Needing to put a specific beat on a specific page may lead to an inauthentic scene for the sake of beat placement, and I feel this is unnecessary and potentially a story killer. In my design I prefer page ranges and have indicated them in the graph below.

One of the common themes in my structural design and character design is symmetry. I believe in balance. Great evil should be balanced by great good. Beats work this way as well. Many of the beats in my screenplays have opposing beats and I discussed this earlier as a symmetry of opposites and poetic balance.

Beat One: The Beginning

You should know this before you begin writing—remember? The very beginning of a film should show the world as the protagonist sees it. Vogler calls this the ordinary world. I think that is fair. This is how things exist before, but the word ordinary is subjective. It only means that it is the world the protag lives in before their choices and actions change things. I call this the OLD WORLD. The first shot in the beginning is symmetrical opposite of the last shot in the ending that shows the world as it has become. I describe them as bookends

Beat Structure Approach

Old World   Upsidedown   New World

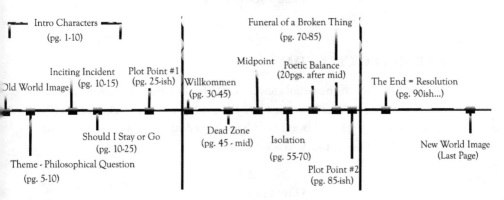

Fig. 4. Beat Structure

that create context and a frame for your story. It allows you the writer to see the entirety of the world and its boundaries.

The first and last shot should be opposites of one another. One shows the world of the protagonist before their conflict and the other shows the world after. McKee calls this the thetical world and the antithetical world, Field as the first half and the second half, it's all the same. Where do you begin, where do you end? Focusing on beats, however, makes this easier for me. I see them as shots, pictures, and visuals. For example, the world before an apocalypse and the world after. This example is mundane and a bit cliché, but does the trick nicely. Let's try it.

FIRST SCENE:

EXT. METRO CITY – DAY

The skyline is beautiful from the hill. MIKE (30s), a handsome rugged bloke, wears khakis and a button-up shirt. A fit manager in a big box retail store. He stares, smiling. He must love this city.

> MIKE
> I love this city.

He wraps his arms around BETH (30s), a librarian type that's a demure nine out of ten.

> BETH
> I know you do, Sparky.

LAST SCENE:

EXT. METRO CITY – DAY

The skyline is not the beautiful view it used to be. Buildings are crumbling and scorched, and smoke still streams into the air. Mike wears black special OPs leather, sports a grizzled beard, and has a sawed-off shotgun slung over his shoulder. He stares at the destruction. He loved this city.

> MIKE
> I loved this city.

Beth, now in matching leather—lady badass outfit—sinks her ninja sword into the ground. Her face is dirty and she has a long scar running from mouth to eye.

> BETH
> I know you did, Sparky.

> FADE OUT.

Attach Bruce Willis and Angelina Jolie and this is a box office crusher! Remember that bookends provide you with the frame into which your entire story will fit and it shows a visual representation to the story arc. Your first shot is of the Old World and should happen very close to page one.

Beat Two: Introduce Your Main Characters

Specifically, your protagonist needs to be developed quickly during the first ten pages. The audience needs to like them or hate them and understand who they are NOW, before the *shite* hits the proverbial fan. There will be a lot of character development that goes beyond this point and you should in no way limit your character development to ten pages, but the idea is that you already know your characters and should be able to execute a full introduction by displaying their personality and flaws without delay. After ten pages your readers may give up on you if you haven't given them some red meat to chew on. Remember that your protagonist is the vehicle in which your story will be moving. They need to be complex and interesting. I would suggest using the archetypes definition here to help introduce them quickly (in a later chapter).

Beat Three: Theme (A Philosophical Question Asked of the Protagonist)

This is the question that I really like to pose, not only to the protagonist, but to the audience. It's the thing that the reader or the audience will go home with. We discussed the importance of this in a previous chapter. This is a philosophical debate that allows readers and audience members to relate to the work in some way that goes well beyond the story. The implications should go deeper, even if you are writing a playful and nonserious film. I encourage you to go back to the great films and find the theme beat. Think of Marcus Aurelius talking to Maximus in *Gladiator*, Neo in *The Matrix*. This question is subconsciously understood by the audience and frames the story rather neatly. In *Home Alone*, Kevin says, "I don't wanna see you again for the rest of my whole life." His mother responds with the thematic line, "I hope you don't mean that. You'd feel pretty sad if you woke up tomorrow morning and you didn't have a family." Hence, the foundation is set and we all wonder what would happen if we got what we wished for. There are those that would say this is unnecessary as a singled-out beat, but I think that films without a specific theme fail to capitalize on the experience of the audience. Blake Snyder says that this beat goes on page five. I don't think that it needs to be so specific, and trying to squeeze it in may make your writing feel forced; however, I do think that the theme beat fits snugly within the first ten pages of your script. If you miss it, the audience will fail to be active in the search for meaning as it relates to them personally. Theme is an interactive element. The reader needs to have the question asked of them early. It is a bit of emotional foreshadowing that prepares everyone for a wild ride. Good news, you already know your theme from earlier. All you have to do is figure out how to present it.

Beat Four: The Inciting Incident

It's hard to get around this one. If nothing happens to start the film, the story is over before it begins. This is the part of the script that forces your protagonist to make a choice. Something lands in their lap and they have to make a decision. There is no option to be neutral. For example, your protagonist receives a phone call saying that an extremely disliked aunt passes away and her will requests that you dispose of her ashes. This is the moment where the film really begins. Snyder calls this the catalyst and says that it goes on page twelve. Once again, I'm not in total agreement. Depending on your script it may be page eleven or page thirteen (definitely in the first sequence). The flow of your story should provide you with the answer. That being said, if you wait too long, you will lose your audience quickly. Too early and you haven't developed your protagonist enough to increase tension. Once you have established full personalities, it should be evident when something needs to happen. That is where the inciting incident goes.

Beat Five: Should I Stay or Should I Go Now? The Clash

This is an interesting part of the screenplay. You need to keep things going, but at the same time the protagonist has not made a decision yet, and so the story can't move. The protagonist has to have a questioning of self here. Will they accept the challenge or will they not? The point is that everyone knows that they will, or the movie is over, BUT why will they go? Character development is huge at this point. I like to expose character flaws here and allow the decision that the protagonist makes to exploit those flaws. This makes it feel more like real life. We all make decisions based on what we want, but what we want may not be what we need. Truby calls this overall desire. The character is going to act in their best self-interest even if it is not the smartest thing. Allow your characters to lie to themselves, whatever it takes to reveal character and come to a decision.

Try this:

A teen struggles to find a way to pay for college, when she receives a call from a lawyer who says her estranged aunt has passed. She must take her ashes to Ireland and spread them in the sea. If she does this, she gets an inheritance, but the exact amount won't be revealed to her until after she undertakes the trip.

Seems like an easy choice, right? Nope! What we find out in the first ten pages is that this aunt swindled her family out of their savings leaving them broke. Should she stay or should she go? Does she really have a choice? What would you do? The point is that if your audience/reader asks this question, then you GOT 'EM! Of course, we lace this with theme as well: is it too good to be true? Another question that gets the audience invested. This is accomplished between pages ten and twenty-five depending on where the inciting incident is placed.

Beat Six: Plot Point One

This is a major beat and it can be found in all three models. It is also one of the four elements that you need to know before you start writing, so this should be an easy write. If plot point one is not executed, act I will dribble into nowhere. This is where the protag makes their choice. "Yes, I hate my aunt who destroyed the family, but she did have money, so I guess I'll go see what the will says. I mean what could happen right?" Well, sorry sport, but now she's an evil ghost who wants your girlfriend's body to possess. Greed is an absolute bitch, ain't it?

Plot point one changes the story's trajectory, and it must be a dramatic action that turns the story upside down. Act I sets up your entire story and it is a short act, so a lot of precise information must be present. Syd Field says, "Act I is dramatic context that holds together dramatic content in Act II and III." In other words, the stuff that happens later in the film makes no sense if it is not set up properly in act I. It is widely accepted that the plot point one beat should land on page twenty-five-*ish*. This gives you time to allow the protagonist's action to take place. Make sure this is a decision and action of the protagonist alone. They can have help, but it needs to be on their shoulders. In my film *Devolve Babylon*, my protagonist, David, must choose whether to leave his old life or not. He is invited into a house that represents act II, the upside down. I have a close shot of his foot stepping over the threshold into act II. He makes the choice to go in and we SEE it. Welcome, David Babylon, to ACT II. Make your character's plot point one choice actionable and visual, and you will have a winner.

Beat Seven: *Willkommen* (Welcome) to Act II

This beat is a large chunk of prose of approximately fifteen pages (same as a sequence) that establishes the upside down world. In classical design this is where you would introduce your B character, a.k.a. the love interest. Also a real nice place to drop some nuggets of wisdom for your protag to use later. The

B character or mentor can spit out something important that seems relatively innocuous but serves as sage advice later on in act III. Sometimes this is the best place to introduce your chief antagonist as well. Once again it depends on the flow of your script. Your protagonist has acquired a challenge and accepted it, and now meets their first obstacle after accepting the challenge, although it may not seem like one as of yet. A dramatic question will be posed to them at this point in the story, the answer to which they will need to have to be successful in the final act.

Beat Eight: The Dead Zone

It is somewhere in the next ten to fifteen pages that I want to hang myself. Act II is an absolute beast to tackle and where most scripts go to die. You can get through this by concentrating on putting your trailer moments here. If it's funny, put lots of funny, scary lots of scary, sexy lots of sex. I'm sure you get it. Blake Snyder says that this is the section that he puts all of his set pieces; he calls it the Promise of the Premise. Remember that "what if" question we talked about earlier? This is a section that delivers on that "what if" question. The problem is that this section really doesn't push the story forward. It's like taking a time out from the story and allowing the protagonist to build false confidence, gather their team, blah blah blah. Your protagonist is putting a plan together, but their plan sucks and is doomed to fail. This section is hard to fill up, but you have to be aiming for the midpoint. My best advice here is to have more ideas than you need. Throw them all up against the wall and see which ones work. Keep the ones that do and cut the ones that don't. Another thing that you can do is go back and see which characters you haven't fully developed yet and get that done here. In my own scripts it is this section that often needs the most attention during the rewrite.

John Truby uses the bad guy here. He likes to reveal, at least in part, the baddie's desire. Later we will discuss character functions. This is important. The antagonist should have a motive that directly opposes the protagonist, but it doesn't have to be personal or directly aimed at the protagonist. Perhaps it becomes personal later, but keep function in mind as you write this section. John Truby also likes to launch the baddie's first attack in this section. I don't disagree, but it depends on your story and screenplay. If you hit a wall, give it a try. Last, don't forget about theme. When you start dragging, consider circling back to theme and hit a dramatic moment that will carry into act III. If you introduce theme correctly in act I it will feel good and not forced. Ideally this happens between pages forty-five and sixty, but it really depends on the length of the script. Aim for the midpoint whether it is page sixty or forty-five.

Beat Nine: Midpoint

Finally, we are back to telling a story. "Broken half in two" (Anthony Michael Hall in *Weird Science*). You have thrown some obstacles at your protagonist. If you have done this correctly you will be feeling the increase in tension, which will result in a pseudo climax. A *fugazi*! Here's where my idea of "symmetry of opposites" comes in. At this midpoint the protagonist has to experience a victory or a defeat, but it is the opposite of what it seems, which will be discovered later. Christopher Vogler in the Hero's Journey describes this as an ordeal and a big change. John Truby has the protag driving here, with an attack by an ally and an apparent defeat. Truby's protag makes a choice that causes a consequence, which seems like a loss, but later there is a reversal. Blake Snyder calls this a false high or a false low. For example, your character Tom is in a rush to get off the plane, rent a car, and get to the meeting on time, but the man in front of him in line rents the last car. He misses his important meeting and there are consequences. "Dang!" Twenty pages later or so, we find out that the car had a bomb inside and killed the driver, but not our protag. "Hooray!" Dramatic irony at its best. This is important, because your protag needs to be defeated or humiliated. The experience makes them grow and allows them to make different decisions later on. No pain, no gain. Allow me to take another moment to drive home the need that you as a writer put your characters under great stress. Without difficulty they cannot magically grow. If they do not experience pain, when they make good decisions later it will not feel as if they have learned anything from the audience's perspective. You will lose them. Don't let your protag off the hook.

Beat Ten: Isolation

Things fall apart now. In every good film this is where your hero decides that they don't need anyone, don't want anyone, or don't deserve anyone. Remember that first really bad break-up in high school and your mom or dad came in to comfort you, but you threw a pillow at them and told them to get out, but really you wanted them to hug you? That's this moment. The protag pushes everyone away. All the plans have failed. The fight is being lost. There seems to be no way forward. Your hero hits the bottom of the well and the clock is ticking. It is that moment where they may want to run away or quit. We have all had these moments in real life, so we can relate, and remember that is half the battle here. Relate to your audience and tap into real life experiences that feel real to them. Here's where the protag becomes their own worst enemy. Meanwhile, back at the ranch, the bad guys are getting their collective *shite* together. Everything is working on all cylinders. They've got the girl, the cool jacket, and the codes to the nuclear bomb. All is good in bad-guy-ville.

Beat Eleven: Poetic Balance

This is the moment where we write the opposing midpoint beat giving balance to our little world. Remember our rent-a-car man scenario? Yeah, your protagonist has been pissed all this time that he had to take a train, because the jerk in front of him rented the last car and he missed the meeting. Well, now the train stops, because the car blew up right on the tracks. Close one! This moment has to make the protagonist think, and they do, which allows them to have a reversal. Truby identifies this as a change of desire or motive. I like to think of it as a growing moment. Your character just had a close one and gosh darn it, things are just-a changin'. Your hero comes to understand that they may have handled everything wrong. They must look at the problem differently and make different decisions. This may seem like a small thing, but it allows for exponential character growth and perspective change. This can be as nuanced as you want, but don't miss it. I like to have this beat happen no more than twenty pages after the midpoint (wherever your midpoint lands). Any more than that and you risk losing the audience. Real growth may take years, but in Hollywood we have roughly two hours, so get on with it.

Beat Twelve: Dealing with the Funeral of a Broken Thing

Blake Snyder believes that this is the appropriate place for the "whiff of death." This is a moment where something or someone dies. A symbolic death shows how out of control we are in the world. It forces the audience to face mortality right along with the protagonist. It screams, "Hey, we're all gonna die, so why not do something good?" Think about the plant dying in *E.T.* It made us all think and helped us access the emotion of that moment. It is an incredibly useful beat that can be underplayed well. If you watch any super hero film (chances are you have, because that is all that is screening nowadays), you will see this moment. An important character to the hero dies and then they gather their angry strength and destroy New York City with their rage. Perhaps underplaying this beat gives it more strength. Imagine a single mother who has pushed away her friends and family, and her house is about to be foreclosed on. She gets a phone call and her son was in a fight at school. As she walks out, a plate falls off the shelf. It was her grandmother's. It was the last material thing she had of hers. Welcome to rock bottom. This is a strong symbolic moment of a broken thing, and it can have just as much of an impact as a main character dying. As a matter of fact, I will go one step further and say that if you have a character die in your script, make them stay dead. Death is permanent and when you make death impermanent the stakes of a story cannot go any higher. And by the way, those dead characters in comic book movies always come back—always, sometimes anyway. Perhaps one of the reasons this genre is not as strong as it once was. Story is sacrificed for the necessity of a franchise. If you kill or break something, it stays broken, dead, or forever changed.

Now that your protag has hit bottom, dealt with a broken thing, they have to recall the advice they received earlier in the movie. You may have put this at the front of act II or elsewhere, either way this is where it matters. This is the weight on the other side of the scale. Advice delivered earlier is now relevant. Once again let me make my case for theme. If you have nothing, circling back to a thematic premise here may be useful. If you have something more active, that is even better. Linda Seger's story spine labels this as the second turning point. That is about as simple as it gets. The protag has come to a point where they must turn left or right. No prevaricating. It is time to grow up and put your big boy or big girl pants on. This is kind of like that moment in WWF wrestling during the 1980s where the crowd starts stomping and clapping and inexplicably gives strength to the wrestler who is all but dead. Just like that, except way different. I think you get it. The protag has to get their *shite* together.

Beat Thirteen: Plot Point Two

Here we are at a tipping point. Your protagonist has accepted a challenge, overcome obstacles, but has been beaten, isolated, and hit rock bottom. They have also learned from their mistakes and begun to understand the advice that was given to them. What will they do with it? Hopefully, you already know, because this is one of the four things you need to know before you begin writing. I can't express any more importantly that this is a choice that the protag has to make on their own and it must be an ACTION, and that action is always best if it is expressed visually. Another thing that forces this choice is that the story lines often converge here. Linda Seger describes this as the second turning and shows it in her story spine as the subplot (B) and the plot (A) realigning into a single trajectory. Through lines will meet here, the internal and external tension, want and need coalesce, etc. It doesn't matter how you describe it or what terms you use. This is a plot point where the main character has to do something, or the story stops dead in its tracks.

John Truby says that "character is action." All the intimate details and archetypes aside, a character on screen will be judged solely on their actions. This is a little like the real world, isn't it? If a person says one thing and consistently does another, aren't they the other thing? Your protag has to do something, and that actionable choice brings us into act III.

Let's try it:

INT. GOOD GUY HQ – DAY

The headquarters look like they have been torn apart by gunfire. Computers are smashed and doors off their hinges. A ragtag group of heavily armed PEOPLE appear tired and hopeless. Soot on their faces, smeared blood, and disappointed eyes. One of them is SAM (30s), the most badass woman on the planet. She nurses a bloody lip.

In walks a man on a mission, AGENT KING (30s). He's been beaten down, but he's made a choice. The group gasps.

> SAM
> You're back.

> AGENT KING
> I know that I have let you all down. But,
> I've made a choice.

He loads his giant handgun. He's ready to kick some bad guy butt.

> AGENT KING
> Let's go kick some bad guy butt.

Sam's eye twinkle. She loves it when he talks tough.

> SAM
>
> You know I love it when you talk tough.

Sam wipes her lip a final time and racks the slide on her gun.
She looks at the group and they all nod in agreement.

> SAM
>
> We're with you, Agent King.
> Right into act three.

It's an action movie with heart. Attach Bruce Willis and Angelina Jolie, and it's a box office crusher. This plot point goes on the tail end of act II and literally pushes us into act III, which is the New World. During the first draft I would be sure that you have a definitive action by your protag. Later you can cut and trim to get it into the best place, but it is more important at this point that you have the beat rather than try to place it perfectly.

Beat Fourteen: The End

Here we are at the climax of the film, and you should already know what happens here as it is one of the four things you should know before writing. The final battle. The point where everything comes together. Many, including McKee, call it Resolution. Vogler describes it as the final attempt, a resurrection where the hero has returned to the ordinary world. John Truby explains it as a new equilibrium. I call it the end. Yes, it's a little simple, but it is the truth. Things are indeed resolved; however, I am always unsure if the hero should win or lose. Hollywood likes winners, so there's that, but what is best for the story? Ultimately what you are going for in this act is the resolution of conflict, both internal and external, both A stories and B stories. The ending must be satisfying and the hero winning or losing has no real bearing on that. Stay focused on what the story calls for. Resolution is in itself resolution.

While the plot and subplots are resolved, I always find it interesting to imply new tensions. Remember when we discussed poetic balance? Well that comes into play here. Remember this, the protag had to change to have a chance at winning. Often change means that their actions have consequences. Even if these are the slightest of internal conflicts, they are new, because of the resolution. Think about competing against a friend for a job, in softball, at Scrabble, whatever. You want to win and may use what you know about them to do so. All is fair right? Maybe so, but this will change things, won't it? That's right, we all have to pay for our choices, both good and bad. Even Batman has to pay for being a hero. He gets old, is broken, and is in pain. Consequences for the common good, but he pays them. This poetic balance adds a layer of truth to your ending that makes it more satisfying, whether the hero wins or loses. Remember earlier I made a reference to *Hunger Games* and Katniss? To win, she not only had to kill, but she had to pretend to fall in love with Peeta—live on TV. *"Yeah*, she cheated death and afforded an impetus to a revolution!" BUT, she also had to go home and deal with her boyfriend Gale Hawthorne played by Liam Hemsworth. *Awkward.* There are consequences to choices, and they must be paid or the story feels inauthentic.

I think it is also important to visually show the audience the New World. It is opposite of the beginning, because that world does not exist any longer. There is no going back. If you have been taking good notes, you will recall that I called the first shot and last shot bookends. For me this provides a frame for my world. It makes the nebulous story parameters finite. I can work with that. You should know this ending and have this visual in mind before you write word one. I promise it will help, even if it changes later. Incidentally it is one of the four things you should know before writing. In retrospect knowing these things really comes in handy, don't it? *Drop mic.*

If you noticed, I did not really include page numbers on the beats. This is because I have come to understand that they hinder more than help. Targeting a beat to a certain page takes away the power of story rhythm. I am always amazed at how well I do when I just write. You can always go back and edit. Let me change that, you WILL go back and edit and rewrite. However, perhaps having an idea may help. Here are some general structural rules that almost everyone agrees on, no matter what structure design you use.

- You need to set up your main character in the first ten pages.
- The inciting incident, catalyst, or dramatic question should happen in the first sequence or between pages ten and fifteen.
- Plot point one needs to be in the end of act I or around page twenty-five.
- Mid-point is the center of your story approximately page forty-five – sixty depending on the length. I shouldn't have to define middle, but I have been watching a good deal of *Archer* lately and I don't trust in subtlety.
- Plot point two needs to be at the end of act II or around page eighty-five.

I can't be any more clear that the page numbers may change. Precisely placed beats on specific pages are all well and good if you have a 110- to 120-page script, but if your script is 90 pages, there will be dramatic differences. Think of the beats I discussed as necessary elements that must take place. When you go back and read it, they should be clear as to the positioning. There is a rhythm to screenwriting, and you need to get in touch with it to feel when these beats need to happen. If you get the four things (beginning, plot point one, plot point two, ending) correct, much of this will fall into place.

Exercise: Pull up the four important things you wrote down at the beginning of the chapter. How did you do? Rewrite them now. A visual beginning and ending (old world and new world), as well as plot point one and two (these should be choices resulting in actions). Make sure you know these cold.

CHAPTER 5

Weeks 7–8: Character, Part I (Intimacy)

Exercise: List two things about your protagonist and antagonist. 1. Something they want everyone to know about them. 2. Something they want no one to know about them.

Now we move to the who. Who is your story about? I have a little bit of a different approach to characters. Combinations of archetypal motivations, flaws, unreliable perspective, and function. The combinations of these elements allow me to build characters that sometimes create tension within themselves. Interesting characters engage audiences. People are pretty messed up, even normal, regular boring people—whatever that means. I like characters who have defects and problems that often work against their own best interest (i.e., dysfunction is the new normal). It allows me to create tension when things are slow going plot-wise. Characters who can be part of functional society and be screwed up at the same time are reflective of the real world. I was screening *The Player* in a History of American Screenwriting class and one of my students asked me a question about the characters. "How can they be so messed up and still have jobs?" I said they are functionally broken. My aim is to make at least some of my characters this way. Functional brokenness. Here's how I look at developing ideas into characters who seem like real people.

First, Jungian archetypes are incredibly useful, and I encourage their use as a base. Some of the motifs that Jung points to and that we recognize are the great mother (nature), the great father (God), and the trickster (naughty boy/selfish/the devil). They instantly conjure images, roles, and motivations that we as readers and viewers can infer. These characters require no explanation. Archetypes define themselves very quickly, and when writing for film the less you have to say the better.

The word archetype comes from the combination of original Greek words *archein* and *typos*, the former meaning original and the latter meaning a

pattern. Characters are original patterns. Interesting in its own oxymoronic
way. Jung believed that his twelve archetypes resided in the very subconscious
of humanity, and therefore, we understand the motivations of these mythical
characters as they are categorized using human motivations: ego, soul, and
self. Moreover, he believed that humanity had a collective consciousness and
that this is why we all defined these characters the same way. It is worth your
time to research Jung's writings and discover their core desires, strategies, and
fears to help identify and formulate good characters. I believe this to be a great
place to design broad characters. I will not go into specifics in this text, but the
categorical list of archetypes is:

EGO

The innocent
The orphan
The caregiver
The hero

SOUL

The explorer
The rebel
The lover
The creator

SELF

The jester
The sage
The magician
The ruler

By title alone you can conjure an idea of who these characters might be.
By adding benevolence or malevolence, their character becomes more complex, and then by adding flaws and trauma they become unique. Jung posited
that we contained more than one of these archetypes in our own personality makeup, but one is often dominant. We can increase complexity by adding a second subordinate archetype. Using these foundational elements of

character allows us as writers to create complex characters that are immediately recognizable by an audience.

Second, I believe that characters all have to have specific roles and functions. Functions are often based on the archetype that a character resides within. Third, there needs to be balance and symmetry among them. Each character pushing in one direction should have an opposing character or element pulling in the opposite direction in order to allow for tension and conflict. Let's define *what* characters have *what* functions, and *what* their opposites are.

Let's start with the *protagonist*. I know that we have all heard of different ideas on lead characters, protags, and heroes. Let's keep it simple by understanding what the purpose of the protagonist is. This lead character, whose choices *drive* the plot forward, *wants/needs* something. We can break it down into that simple thing. A protagonist is the lead character who wants/needs something. They may not even know what they want or if what they want is or is not what they need. This is all the good stuff that makes characters interesting, likable, or hate-able. Your protag needs to be driven forward to get something no matter their personality. We all have major and minor motivations; what are theirs? So, what do they want and how does their personality allow them to make choices (good and bad) to achieve their goal? Using an archetype as a foundation to personality and motivation will help.

Here is a *premise*: What if a thirty-something pothead slacker decides to get his stuff together and change his life?

Now let's force them to ascribe to an archetype.

1. As a *hero* they would want to prove to the world that they are more than meets the eye and worthy of praise.
2. As an *explorer* they would desire freedom to find out who they really are beneath their social label.
3. As a *ruler* they would desire control of their world and be forced to step on toes as they moved forward.

These three examples foretell three very different movies. You need to identify what your protagonist wants specifically. This is not usually a general thing. For instance, your protag may want happiness. How? They may want to be happy, but they also want to be happy in a specific way. They may want the girl or guy, to get into an Ivy League college, the promotion, their parent's inheritance—what have you. This should be specific, and then you can subscribe to an archetype that provides some interesting directions and choices for your protag to chase what they want. Your use of archetype will influence how they treat other people and identify a value system for them. Will they lie? Will they screw over their friends? Will they cheat? Good people doing bad things for good reasons is just as interesting as bad people doing good things for bad reasons.

Exercise: Let's take our premise and build a story and plot and see if we can develop an interesting protagonist. I've put an example below. I want you to use an archetype for the protagonist and see if we have a good place to start a screenplay. Change them around as much as you want.

PREMISE: What if a thirty-something pothead slacker decides to get his stuff together and change his life? This protag can be male or female.

ARCHETYPE: Explorer

THEME: Identity. Who am I when I shed my child's skin?

STORY: After the death of his mother, a thirty-year-old slacker decides that he needs to grow up and discover his place in the world.

PLOT: A thirty-year-old slacker living at home wakes up from a bender to find his mother has passed away. Taking the advice of their last conversation, he decides it is time to go out into the world and discover his true purpose and finds himself volunteering in the Peace Corps in Africa.

Using the same premise, change the underlining archetype and build your own protagonist. He or she should feel real to you when you're done.

Intimacy

Let's say you are unsure how to get to know your character. What do you do? What you have is an intimacy problem. You need to improve your relationship. Think of your first or second date with someone new. What do you want to know, and then what do you really want to know? Different answers for each, hey? Let me tell you about one of my screenwriting classes. A student of mine, Phil Carwane Esq., was already a talented writer, and after this class we worked together for years. He was even an AD on one of my films, *Devolve Babylon*. He asked how I knew my characters so well. After years of writing I was caught off guard and unsure how to answer in an academic way. How the hell *do* I know my characters? Damn it! Unfortunately, I started my answer with, "Well, that's easy Phil...," and then I stood there with my mouth open for a few moments and began to stuff humble pie into it. Had I that class to do over again, I would be more prepared to articulate in a cognizant manner. First, we writers typically create characters from a part of ourselves and bits and pieces of people we know. Some writers use scribble sheets, index cards, or other devices to write down as much as we know about any given character. Once the writing begins we start to really learn this character and get a better feel for them, essentially becoming intimate with them. Not fully being aware of who they are as people means we often have to go back and rewrite because they would never do this or that, so someone else has to do it and that changes the plot device and … yeah we've all been here before. As with all things, really knowing your character before you start writing is the best place to start. Characters with deficient development, cardboard-thin personalities, and a lack of flaws will absolutely kill a good story. Characters unable to execute good stories fail in holding the audience's attention. I would venture to say that TV audiences often decide to continue watching a series based on characters that they love or hate. Great concepts and attachments may get people to tune in, but great characters bring them back. Amazing stories can't be told using average characters. One of the best TV shows I have ever seen is *The Sopranos*. Tony, the protagonist, is a murderer and sociopath, who is developed so well that we empathize with him and cheer for him throughout the series. WTF? A sociopathic gangster and we love him? That is the power of creating a truly complex and relatable character.

I think it's important that you learn how to inhabit a character. You know, really get inside them. This can be a challenge for gender reversals, but good screenwriters can write both sexes well. Frances Marion was not only a stand-out female writer in the Golden Age of film, but perhaps one of the most influential. Marion knew how to inhabit her characters and wrote incredible roles for men. She was so good that she won two Oscars for *The Big House* and *The Champ*. She may have written the first book on screenwriting, *How to Write and Sell Film Stories* (1937).

Here are a few questions that might get you started on knowing who your character is. These aren't the only questions you need to ask yourself, but having these done before you write may be a good start and may lead you to the more probing and relevant questions. Keep in mind the archetypes that you have selected for these characters before you answer, as the answers will most likely change.

1. Where did they grow up?
2. What was their childhood like?

3. Did they go to college or finish high school?
4. Parents, brothers/sisters, and their relationships?
5. Favorite color, food, movie, car (anything relevant)?
6. Age?
7. Physical deformities, disabilities, limitations, limps, chronic pain, etc.?
8. What is a typical day like for this person?
9. Have they been in love, heartbroken?
10. Morals, ethics, standards?
11. Is there anything sacred to them?
12. Memories, good and bad?
13. Sexual proclivities and/or orientation?
14. Life-changing seminal moments?
15. What is their biggest vice (coffee, cigarettes, heroin, sex)?
16. Is that vice secret?
17. Profession or job/unemployed?
18. What type of car do they drive? Is it relevant?
19. Do they wear name-brand or non–name-brand clothing?
20. What are their politics?
21. What are their religious affiliations?
22. Do they have extreme narcissism, selfishness, racism, sexism, violence, patience, intelligence?

As I said, there are so many questions that you can ask, but these are a general good start to becoming intimate with your character(s). Based on these questions answered honestly, you should know within reason how they will respond to situations in your story and why. Keep in mind that your characters will on occasion frustrate you and disappoint you. If this happens it is gold. Real people frustrate and disappoint. Allow these things to happen naturally, and it will if you know them intimately.

Something that I have done quite recently after feeling as if a character needed a bit more development was to give them a personality test. On most occasions I have who my characters are pretty well in mind, but on this occasion I came up short. If you find yourself in this position, try giving the personality test. The two I recommend are the Meyers-Briggs Type Indicator (MBTI) and the Type A, B, C, and D Personalities.

The MBTI works really well with archetypes as it was based on Jung's research. It doesn't matter what you think about the research itself, only that this is a tool to help design interesting and complex characters.

First, how does your character(s) experience the world: introversion or extroversion? Second, does your character use evidence-based information to make decisions or do they interpret information for themselves (sensing, intuition)? Third, does you character make decisions based on logic or special circumstances (thinking, feeling)? Last, when interfacing with the world, does your character make definitive decisions based on their own experience or do they have more of an open mind (judging, perceiving)?

Let's do a for an example: INFJ (introverted, intuition, feeling, judging), the rarest personality at 2 percent of the population. They have a deep sense of personal integrity and intuition making them able to interpret other people's emotions and motivations easily. They are fairly idealistic and prefer a small groups of friends that contain deep connections rather than large groups of superficial connections. They are often quiet and gentle, and continued social contact can exhaust them. Does this personality type fit your character? Do the restrictions make things more interesting? Remember it is all up to you.

There are many websites available for you to discover these personality types, however, what I find most useful is that as a writer you ask yourself these questions. Each question answered allows for an additional layer of an interesting person. Make sure to write these down so that you can stay consistent over the course of the screenplay.

A more simple personality check may be the four types. Most of us understand what an A Type personality person is. The overachiever and natural leader (or wannabe), who wants to be in control as much as possible. This could be a good trait or bad as long as it's consistent.

The B Type is a peacemaker, a bridge builder. Type B personalities are diametrically opposed to A types. They are outgoing and enjoyable to be around in positive situations, but may have needy inclinations.

Type C personalities are similar to Type A in their focus on details, accuracy, and control, but are more introverted. Think of them as a thinker or analyst who uses logic to make sense of the world. Situations that don't go to plan can overwhelm them, especially when they aren't in control.

Type D personalities are similar to B Types and are sometimes categorized as philosophers. They are in touch with their emotions and experience joy and happiness more intensely than others. The catch is that they are also more easily anxious and depressed as well.

Using one or both of these tools may help you construct a more complex character. Remember that you should be thinking of your characters as real human beings. If you do, so will the people who read your script. Characters are the vehicles that stories are told through, and without a good one your script is dead on arrival.

HINT: Keep in mind that every character in your story believes that they are the protagonist. If you approach character building from this vantage, you will design a much more authentically human character.

CHAPTER 6

Weeks 9–10: Character, Part II (Functions)

Exercise: Who is the third most important character in your screenplay? Explain what it is that they do. In other words, what is their precise function related to the protagonist?

Let's talk about functions. A good screenplay can have one character, or it can have twenty. The number of characters is only relevant to STORY. Having said that, there are some things you should know about properly balancing your characters. Jungian psychology lists twelve major roles; however, I ascribe to eight main character *functions* that you should think about when writing. Identifying a character's function will tighten your script and make the story more succinct, as well as make your protag's path much clearer. Every functional character in a story should have a specific job as it relates to the protagonist. Identifying the role of character can help focus your plot when properly combined with a character's personality and motivations. In this way it becomes a bit mechanical. Think about it this way: every part in a car engine has a function. Yes, it can operate without some, but not efficiently. Try pulling out the last spark plug. Your car will run and drive, but not very well, spasmodically at best. Screenplays are not much different. If a character is deemed important enough to name, then most likely they should have a specific purpose. If they don't have a purpose (which includes developing the protag's character), cut them. Each character is present to perform a story purpose or to develop another character. If you find a character that does neither of these (and I don't mean WAITRESS #1 or MAN WITH HAT), then you need to step back and see if they are necessary in the story. Remove them and see if they make a difference. If you remove them and it leaves no holes, they should end up on the cutting room floor.

We discussed the protagonist and how they move the story forward by wanting/needing something and relentlessly attempting to get it. The antagonist's job is quite the opposite. They must stop the protagonist from achieving their goal at all costs. It is the primary impetus of conflict. The antagonist has their own motivations, personal, professional, religious, it doesn't matter what you choose it to be, as long as you understand that the nature of their function is to completely oppose. You get to choose the most interesting and specific things about why the antagonist does what they do, but they must *need* to stop the protagonist from achieving their goal. In this way it is a zero-sum game. The protagonist and the antagonist have opposing functions and one cannot live without the other. Every screenplay must have the opposing forces of a protagonist and antagonist, the first two of the eight characters. The old guard would define this as the White Hat Cowboy and the Black Hat Cowboy. Good versus evil, but I dissuade this type of writing. Good guys shouldn't be all that good and bad guys shouldn't be all that bad. It makes for much more interesting characters to mix in flaws. Good guys with addictions, bad guys who love their mothers, you know that ol' chestnut.

The above two characters are necessary; however, all the rest of the characters described below are not. That being said, if you choose one of them, you need the functional other (remember opposing forces), which I will identify as matched pairs. Remember, these functions are opposites and therefore need one another for story balance. The characters below are all based on Jungian archetypes and therefore will be recognized, but for this portion of the writing you should myopically focus on function as related to the protagonist not personality. There is development software available that is designed to assist you in developing characters using these Jungian archetypes, but I believe it to be an important exercise to do so without assistance to understand this process intimately. The process is comprehensive and very specific.

To summarize, we have the protagonist. This character drives the plot forward by trying to achieve a want/need at all costs. The opposite is the antagonist, who will stop the protag at all costs to achieve their goal. The protag and antag do not have to be cognizant of their opposition to one another as long as their actions are directly and diametrically opposed. Let's go through the remaining six character functions.

The *support* character, also known as the sidekick, assists the protagonist in reaching their goal, whether it is a good goal or not. They are most often a faithful servant (Alfred in the original version of *Batman*). The support character has inexhaustible loyalty. Their fidelity lends the protagonist the strength they need to brave their struggles. It is important to mention that the support character does not need to be aligned with the protagonist, but most often is. That's correct, you can use the sidekick as an antagonist ally, however uncommon. The sidekick may show up for a moment or be present throughout. This is not a necessary character in a screenplay, however, if they are present you need to balance the story with the cynic.

The *cynic* is a character that hampers faith. Regardless if they are good or bad, their main function is to throw a monkey wrench into the belief system of the protagonist, no matter if they are aligned with them or not. In other words, it doesn't matter if they are a good guy or bad guy; they perform the same function. They sew doubt on everything from choices to actions, to non-actions—everything. Remember that this is less about which team they play for and more of what is their function. In the cynic's case, it is to hamper and obstruct faith, period. Cynicism is the opposite of faith.

What we have so far is a character trying to get something and a character trying to stop them (protag/antag). A character lending full faith and a character impeding that faith (support/cynic). Sounds fairly balanced to me. Next on our list is the *teacher* and the *contagonist*. I really enjoy that last term and learned about it from the Dramatica team. I felt it was the best one-word moniker that appropriately attributed to the function of this Jungian Loki/trickster type character.

The *teacher* acts like the good conscious of the protagonist. Remember the angel and the devil that would sit on Tom's shoulder from the *Tom & Jerry* cartoon? Yeah, that guy. It is the white-clad angel on the right shoulder whispering wisdom into the ear of the protagonist. It provides guidance and help, usually necessary in act III, and is useful in establishing *theme*, which I think is absolutely necessary to a satisfying story. Think Mick in *Rocky* or Obi Wan Kenobi in *Star Wars*. Guidance and wisdom come from this character with the sole function of giving the protagonist the lesson they may need to win the final battle. A protag needs to change in a story, and this lesson from the teacher provides a foundation for that change. Many times the teacher will be a priest or religious figure. It may not be that the protagonist subscribes to the same value system as the teacher, but the universal sense of ethics and morality help center them and provide them with global knowledge to use, not necessarily to defeat the antagonist, but to achieve their goal. Remember that the function of a protagonist is not always to defeat the antagonist, but to achieve their goal, and the antagonist is merely an obstacle.

To balance this character, we have the *contagonist*. I just love this character's function, because it can be used to really simulate the randomness of real life. The contagonist character doesn't require a personal stake in whatever is going on. I personally like to use this character as connected to the external tension. This character is a real wild card and often hinders the protagonist using confusion and chaos, but it can affect everyone simultaneously. This is the devil on Tom's left shoulder, or at least as close as you get to that. The Wizard in *The Wizard of Oz* is the contagonist, as he delays Dorothy for his own ends. He isn't against her or for the Witch, he just has his own agenda and that happens to be against both Dorothy and the Witch, although it has nothing to do with either. This character can be used to amazing ends as completely disconnected from both the A and B story lines. Do not underestimate the use for them.

EXT. DUSTY STREET – DAY

High noon scorches the dirt road leaving dry wagon tracks visible. Horses tied to posts drink deeply from troughs of water.
BLACK HAT (30s) stands in the center of the street, dirty, afraid, eyes as large as saucers. Sweat beads off his scruffy face.
His fingers tap the butt of a pistol at his side.
WHITE HAT (30s) stands looking relaxed. The sun doesn't seem to touch him.

> WHITE HAT
> It's over. No more running. It's time to give it up.

> BLACK HAT
> You know I ain't going back to jail.

> WHITE HAT
> I was hoping you'd say that.

White Hat stands straighter, ready. The air must have changed, as onlookers rush into the safety of their wooden shops.

In a flash White Hat draws his pistol, clearly outgunning Black Hat, but at the same time an EXPLOSION interrupts the gun fight and White Hat's shot goes wide.

A horse rears back and runs, knocking White Hat to the ground. White Hat gets up, panicked, gun drawn, but Black Hat is nowhere to be seen. He's escaped.

A fire burns the bank behind him. Out of the front door steps a MASKED man wearing a GRAY HAT and holding a bag of money. He locks eyes for a moment with White Hat, but no recognition.

                    WHITE HAT
          Damn you.

                    GRAY HAT
          Me? What I do?

Gray Hat gets on his horse and rides away leaving White Hat alone in the street.
                    WHITE HAT
          (Melodramatically)
          Nooooo.

In this scene we can clearly see how the Gray Hat contagonist can serve our story. They may know what they are doing or they may not. Your choice; however, without the use of a fully developed contagonist this would be far too convenient. We've seen this in bad movies, but with a developed character who has an agenda of their own, which happens to cross paths with the main tension, it adds a third dimension to the story and adds that randomness of life that feels authentic. Chaos and confusion are the best weapons in the contagonist's arsenal, and they may not even know the damage that they are doing to the other characters. TV writers do this well. This is the C story, a disconnected plot line that comes into conflict with the A story.

The next pair of characters are about hearts and minds. The *emotional* character and the *logical* character. These two are exactly what they sound like. One reacts with pure emotion and the other acts with pure logic. The lack of reactive flexibility allows us to place these characters in situations that present wonderful tension for the protagonist. Once again it doesn't matter which team they play for, only that they provide a congruity to the story. These characters provide either the emotional push the protag needs or the emotional explosion that they don't. The logic character provides the facts they need to hear or the truth they don't want to. It doesn't matter, only that if you have one you should have the other.

You may choose to have some of these characters only briefly appear. Except for the protagonist and antagonist, that is just fine. As long as they fulfill their function, it is fine. Remember this is about function not personality. For example, the logic character doesn't have to have a logical personality, but the way they interface and affect the protagonist must be in a logic-based way. Same goes for the teacher; they don't need to be a teacher-type, only a person who helps the protag learn something they need to and so on and so forth. The longer a character stays in a piece, the more complexity the audience is going to expect out of them. Using the combination of archetypes, personalities, and functional roles will allow you to build solid and satisfying characters for your story.

To sum this up, we writers must create complex characters to make stories feel real. Archetypes are very useful in building realistic, instantly recognizable characters; however, we must realize that human beings are rarely so identifiable. We use archetypes to reduce the need for exposition, but we must constantly look for opportunities to add layers of complexity, hence the personality types. The intricate nature of humanity creates obstacles to climb knowingly and unknowingly. We have to realize that in stories characters have function and these jobs help the protagonist push the story forward by learning lessons, dealing with emotions from disappointment to great joy, dealing with unexpected events, and ultimately changing enough to win (or lose).

CHAPTER 7

Weeks 11–12: Dialog

Exercise: A man and woman are eating dinner at a fine establishment. One is cheating on the other and one wants a divorce. Neither knows about the other. Write a one-page scene that would allow a viewing audience to understand what is going on in the minds of the characters without them saying it directly. No expository dialog!

What Do I Say: Dialog

What the hell do I say now? Dialog can be a bear. It is most often used incorrectly as a vehicle for the exposition of information. This is not what dialog is for. Remember that this is a visual medium. We should be able to watch a film on mute and still know what is going on. If that is true, what is dialog for? Good question. Character. When you go on a date or out to dinner with new people, you listen to what they say closely. Unless you're a narcissist of course, and then you don't give a damn what they say unless it has to do with you. Ignoring that fact, people describe who they are through dialog. They may not know it, but they do. Even if people say the opposite of who they are, that says a lot about them as well, right? What they say, how they say it, and what they *don't* say is a development tool for character.

In film, we show, don't tell, so what *do* we tell? We tell the audience who the characters are and we show them what they are doing and how they push the plot. Dialog serves to help us decide why a character is doing what they are doing. It gives us insight into their flaws and motivations, which adds a layer of intrigue to the film. This has nothing to do with genre. In comedy it may be even more important to flesh out a character. Let's try this:

STUDENT: What should my character say?

PROFESSOR: What are they doing?

STUDENT: Nothing.

PROFESSOR: They have to do something.

STUDENT: What does that have to do with what they say?

PROFESSOR: Nothing, but they can't say what they're doing.

STUDENT: But they're not doing anything.

PROFESSOR: Exactly.

You have to have a clear understanding of your plot so that you don't inadvertently tell the audience in a grand display of exposition. It's a real letdown when that happens. So once you figure out how your character will take action and move the plot forward, you can devise dialog that identifies their character.

Dialog is also tricky, because human beings do not often say exactly what they want to say. Your significant other asks you what you want for Christmas. You say, "I don't know, nothing I guess." However, you really know that you want the brand-new iPhone XX with the reality-bending dimensional shift portal app. So, why did you say nothing? We do not say what we mean all of the time for any number of reasons. Your boss comes to you at work and stops by your desk. "How is it going? Any problems in the workplace I can help you with?" You smile and shake your head. "No, boss. Everything is just peachy." However, the guy in the next cubicle comes to work thirty minutes late every day, takes four twenty-minute bathroom breaks and a two-hour lunch, and you have to do all of his work. What do you do? You go home and bitch to your mom about how work sucks! We rarely say what we mean. Try this:

STUDENT: What should my character say?

PROFESSOR: What are they doing?

STUDENT: Robbing a bank.

PROFESSOR: Don't talk about robbing the bank.

STUDENT: But they are robbing a bank.

PROFESSOR: Of course they are. Don't say what they mean, but mean what they say.

STUDENT: What do you mean?

PROFESSOR: Exactly!

Characters in the middle of robbing a bank could easily talk about jobs that they have done previously, the best new first-person shooter game, their home life, or the new hair product they are using. Any one of these ridiculous subjects would provide us with incredible insight into these characters. Be creative.

Recently in my Master Screenwriting class we were reading a dialog-heavy scene. It was good and did a fine job of character development. For some reason the scene felt flat, boring, uninteresting. This was weird because the dialog was good. Bobby Bowman (*Family Guy*) threw out a note he called "pestered by a bee." Basically, this was a way to add a visual to the dialog that ginned up tension, as well as further developed character. It could also be used to push plot forward simultaneously. I stole this and made it my own. I call it SWATTING THE BEE. Thanks Bobby.

Here-s an example:

EXT. SIDEWALK – NIGHT

TONYA (30s) and JESSIE (30s) talk on the sidewalk in front of Tonya's apartment building. Tonya looks a bit down.

> TONYA
> I just feel it deep down in my bones.
> It seems so obvious.

> JESSIE
> He loves you. I don't think he'd cheat.

> TONYA
> He's a man, ain't he?

They both laugh and hug.

> TONYA
> I guess you're right. Night.

Feeling better, Tonya walks towards her apartment door and waves goodbye to Jessie.

> FADE OUT.

This conversation is boring, although it's important information for the audience to learn. If we swat the bee here, we can make a lot more happen and make it entertaining.

EXT. SIDEWALK – NIGHT

TONYA (30s) and JESSIE (30s) talk on the sidewalk in front of Tonya's apartment building. Only one window has a light on in the building. No curtains. Tonya looks a bit down in the dumps.

> TONYA
> I just feel it deep down in my bones.
> It seems so obvious.

A couple can be seen KISSING in the throes of passion through the window.

> JESSIE
> He loves you. I don't think he'd cheat.

The MAN looks out the window and sees the two women talking. His eyes seem to bulge in SHOCK.

> TONYA
> He's a man, ain't he?

They both laugh and hug.

He PULLS his LOVER away from the window in a hurry and a moment later the light goes OUT.

> TONYA
> I guess you're right. Night.

Feeling better, Tonya walks towards her apartment door and waves goodbye to Jessie.

> FADE OUT.

Written this way the dialog is much more entertaining, and the visual elements allow the story to move forward. When your dialog begins to sag, look for an opportunity to *swat the bee*.

We don't communicate clearly in the real world and neither should your characters. Remember that we often communicate feelings and emotions badly, more than we communicate information. When characters communicate unimportant information badly to one another, it can be brilliant and engaging dialog.

CHAPTER 8

Weeks 13–14: Rewriting

Where to begin and where to end? Rewriting is a skill unto itself. It requires a great amount of objectivity and trust. I have often tried to codify a way to attack the rewrite process for efficiency and effectiveness. Unfortunately, I have found that every script is a battle completely unique of others. So where should you begin? This chapter focuses on rewriting your own script, not someone else's, so please keep that in mind as you move forward, although generally the process is the same. Let's try to get you going in the correct direction.

First and foremost, put your script down. You need separation. You need time. Take a month or a couple weeks off. If you are writing within a semester this changes completely and you are on a much shorter clock. You still need to give your mind a break. Take as much time as you can—don't peek! You need to get your eyes off the script. Watch some movies you like, read a book, do something to change your eye line and give you some perspective. I would suggest watching a *good* movie or reading a *good* book, because you want examples that have good rhythm before you go back to your own work.

Second, after your break read your script all the way through. My advice is to print it out. You're going to want to make changes immediately, but I would encourage you to read it all the way through. If you don't have the discipline (like me), you can write your notes directly on the script. I know it is a pain to print a hundred or so pages. I know it is a pain to carry it around; however, it is my experience that when it is a physical thing it somehow creates more value. Read it all the way through and only jot down notes. You need to do this in one sitting. It is important that you feel the rhythm of the story. There are some who say you need to take a walk now, chew on the story, and reflect on it. Not a bad idea, but in most cases I get right to work. I'm also impetuous. Try discipline if you can. There is no correct answer here, except when the final is due. Whether a producer wants a delivery date or a professor an assignment due date, you need to be able to have a little space from the story. Read it objectively, and begin to find its faults. If you are trying to complete this feature for a final assignment, time is short by now, so you need to get on the stick. Here are the steps I take to make sure I hit all the marks.

Structure

Dialog is going to stick out like a sore thumb, but structure is first for me. The framework needs to be solid and having things in their proper places sometimes fixes dialog—well sort of. Focus on the macro, big pieces, and work your way down. Did the timing feel off or the read get boring, was it slow in places? The story needs to have a sense that it is falling forward and increasing in velocity. If it doesn't this is most likely a structure issue. Remember premise? Does this question get answered and connect the beginning with the end? Go back to chapter 4 and reacquaint yourself with the elements of structure, and then see what you missed. Identify the big four: beginning, plot point one, plot point two, and the end. Are they reminiscent of the story? Acts I, II, and III—the Old World, the Upside Down World, and the New World. Can you visualize the change in each act to represent these descriptions? Whether you are using the sequencing method, basic three act, or a beat sheet, be sure that everything is where it is supposed to be. One misplaced beat or plot point can throw an entire script off its axis.

If things continue to feel slow, try moving scenes around or cut them. Does everything make sense? Does the audience have the information they need, or you have intentionally kept information from them to increase anxiety, tension, and drama? Each scene should have a specific reason to be there. Ask yourself what this scene does. Any scene that seems off, read the script without the scene. Did it work? If so, kill it and move on.

Does your protagonist make actionable (visual) choices that push the plot forward, specifically at the plot points? Are they passive or active? Be objective. If they are not DOING, then you need to change that. Your protagonist must make choices that result in action and keep things moving forward. Double check plot points one and two and see what your protag does to remain the driving force. What do they want/need, and are they constantly working toward that objective through visual action? The answers to these questions will help you tweak the structure into a framework designed to keep the script moving. Take a look at your protagonist's through lines. Are they clear? Have you answered the "what if" question all the way through the story? Do the through lines intersect in the third act? The placement of all of these elements should be designed specifically to create tension and pull us toward a final conflict. Remember what William Goldman said: "Screenplays are structure."

Character

Look at the decisions of all your characters. Do their decisions adhere to the values, morals, and ethics that you have designed into their personalities? Inhabit your characters and feel what they feel. Are they consistent all the way through the screenplay? If one of your characters all of a sudden acts differently, there needs to be a reason that we have shown visually and that the audience understands. Have the characters changed or grown? This doesn't only apply to your protagonist. Every character in the story thinks *they* are the protagonist in the story. I don't know who said it, but paraphrased, "Everyone is the main character in their own life." Be sure you know these people and that they are acting accordingly. You may have used the Jungian archetypes to design your characters; if so, consistency is key here. Remember their flaws. Have you exploited their flaws and given them the opportunity to fix them?

Let's go back to chapter 6 and reacquaint ourselves with functions. You may have tasked certain characters with functions. Are they doing their jobs? Are they affecting the protagonist in the way you wanted them to? Now is the time to make sure all of these people are doing their jobs.

Up the Stakes

Every screenwriting book or educator worth their salt will have a version of this statement. Inevitably your screenplay needs more tension and conflict, and consequences for choices made. What if the protagonist fails? What is the consequence? These need to be clear, and if they don't hold enough weight, you need to go back to work. Here are a few ways to do this. Keep in mind that these are only ways in which to think about improving your script. Not every note is executable, but the process of thinking it through is the money. The way I do this is to create limitations for the protagonist.

I believe the first and the one that is most often used incorrectly in the first draft is the limitation of time and space. I use the term TIME LOCK and so do many other writers. There are many different terms, but they all mean the same thing. You need to put a limitation on how long your protag has to learn their lessons, change, make amends, design a plan to win, and ultimately meet the final battle. A protag has a goal (want/need) and you need to restrict the time they have to achieve it. For example, any high school movie has a built-in time lock: prom night, summer, final exams, college application deadlines. In any one of these cases the protag has to achieve their goal by this naturally occurring time limitation. Of course we have the bomb countdown and the ransom time line, but the more natural the time lock is, the better it will feel in your movie. The second piece of this is limited space. Ninety-nine percent of the time you have to find a way to force your protag to face your antag. Protags can't win passively; they must make a choice and face the music head-on. Finding ways to limit their ability to fight from a distance creates tension— which is gold in a script. A great example of time and space limitations is in Quentin Tarantino's *The Hateful Eight*. The vast majority of the film takes place in the single room of Minnie's Haberdashery. Throughout the course of the story, it becomes very clear that not everyone, and perhaps no one, will make it out of the room alive. The imminent arrival of characters makes time of the essence, as well as the limitation on space forcing characters to confront one another. It makes for excellent tension.

A second way to up the stakes is by limiting allies. In classic screenwriting a character goes through a period of isolation so that they can learn lessons and grow. It is then that they can make amends and get the band back together. Have you done this? Are they isolated enough to force them to make choices that teach them something? Perhaps getting the band back together relieves your script of tension and works against the protag's growth. So it's time to do something else. Perhaps it is time to limit their allies. The protag can lose friends by death, betrayal, argument, and abandonment. In *The Revenant*, Leonardo DiCaprio's character quickly loses all his allies. He moves through the entire story in isolation and loneliness. The more these characters lose, the higher the stakes become. Whether you focus on isolation or the limitation of allies, what matters is what works best for your story. Creating limitations of time, space, or allies are all ways to increase tension and improve the story's stakes and quality.

Getting stuck in the middle. This is common; your script is good, solid, everything seems to be working, but something is missing and you don't quite know what it is. You are stuck. Allan Durand said, "Every five to ten pages,

I wanted a big fist to come out of the screenplay and punch the reader in the gut." That doesn't mean you need explosions or gunfights, but something needs to happen. You don't have any ideas or nothing is popping off the page? Here are four ways to try to get you unstuck.

1. Discredit the character your protag trusts the most. Trust is a contract between two people: you and a friend, a significant other, a parent, etc. If you break that contract, it strikes a serious emotional chord. The same goes for your protagonist. If they learn that a trusted confidant has betrayed them, it puts their zeitgeist in peril and forces them to act. See if this helps up the stakes in the story.

2. Kill a main-*ish* character. The killing of anyone on screen that the audience has grown to know always raises the stakes. It reinvigorates the need for actionable choices. The consequences of those actions are very real, and therefore this can up the stakes. Look for places in the script where things become slow and meandering. This may be a good solve. Think *Game of Thrones,* which did an amazing job of constantly usurping audience expectations.

3. Write the impossible, the improbable, and the impractical. So many films fall into genre traps where the audience knows what is coming. Sometimes it is a very good thing and sometimes it is quite trite. Perhaps it is time to do the impossible. Think of this as an exercise. Write the most impossible thing to give a scene or an action beat a shot of steroids. Don't hold back, experiment. It may be over the top, but it also may lead to a realistic inspiration. Audiences want to be taken by surprise. Is there anything you can do to make their eyebrows raise and add tension?

4. Fix the first act. This is my go-to. When my script slows down, it is usually because I have failed to properly set things up. Billy Wilder said, "If you have a third act problem, it's a first act problem." If you find yourself meandering in the middle of act II that leads to a flat act III, something is wrong with act I. Recheck your structure and active characters, and be sure plot point one is solid. You read act I more than any other act when writing, so it becomes easy to go blind on what it contains. Read it again with a new set of eyes.

These are big (macro) ways to look at the rewriting process, however, once you get the big taken care of, you have to look at the minutia. The little segments that make up a script are scenes, and this is the way that we tell stories. If a script is the human body, scenes are finger and toes. We can operate fine with a broken toe, but if someone steps on it, the whole body goes down. Every scene is important in some way. The protagonist must make choices and DO things, which demonstrate their motivations. The protag should be able to overcome obstacles (many different internal and external) to achieve their goal. The obstacles must be clear and visual. Your protag needs to make sacrifices to achieve these small victories, as well as large ones, and we have to do this without being expository. As Robert McKee said, "If the story you're telling, is the story you're telling, you're in deep shit."

Go to scenes that you think are problematic and ask yourself these questions to make sure your scenes have meaning:

1. What does the protagonist NEED in this scene? Allow us to visually identify what they need and watch them try to attain it.
2. Why do they need it? Each scene allows us to watch the protag act, but we also need the internal why. What is this motivating factor that pushes the need?
3. What ACTION do they take to get it? This is easy: what do they do? What exact actions do they take? Door #1 or door #2.
4. What is the conflict in their way? Stories are about conflict. Protags must face significant opposition to attain what they need. The conflict often results in character changes that allow the "getting" of need to be accomplished. Pain = growth. Show us how they will be impeded.

Scenes can be broken down into three easy-to-remember parts: Goal, Conflict, and Failure:

Goal

The protag tries to attain a short-term goal. It is active. We understand what it is they want/need and see how they will try to get it and their POV, which helps us understand how they think achieving this will help them in achieving their larger goal.

Conflict

A force or antagonist must try to stop them from attaining this short-term goal. This can lead to additional conflicts with nature or other characters, which makes the plot more complex and human.

Failure

The character must experience failure. There are three general ways to allow a character to fail while maintaining integrity of the scene:

1. They fail to attain a short-term goal. Go back to the drawing board to succeed a second time.
2. They fail to attain a short-term goal and learn of another problem making matters much worse, which increases the tension.
3. They succeed in getting the short-term goal, but success has caused an additional problem.

Which failure model you choose (and you do not have to use one of these) must seem like a direct consequence of trying to succeed at acquiring the goal. It can't be coincidental (DEUS EX MACHINA).

Here's an example: A GOOD man and a BAD man are arguing. BAD is destroying GOOD's family, and in the end GOOD just can't beat him, but a TORNADO shows up and kills BAD. Yay, we win! Except that this sucks.

Each scene needs to feel like it could happen in the world you have created only affected by the CHOICES and ACTIONS of your protag. Remember, as Stephen King said, "In many cases when a reader puts a story aside it is because it 'got boring,' the boredom arose because the writer grew enchanted with his powers of description and lost sight of his priority, which is to keep the ball rolling."

Another place that scenes tend to fall apart is in the beginning of act II. The story seems to slow down in many scripts here. If this is your script, then you may have a set piece problem. According to John August, a set piece is "a scene or sequence with escalated stakes and production values, as appropriate to the genre. For instance, in an action film, a set piece might be a helicopter chase amid skyscrapers. In a musical, a set piece might be a rollerblade dance number. In a high-concept comedy, a set piece might find the claustrophobic hero on an increasingly crowded bus, until he can't take it anymore. Done right, set pieces are moments you remember weeks after seeing a movie." Think of any fighter jet scene in *Top Gun: Maverick*. Now you got it.

There are so many books to tell you how to write a proper set piece, but here is a simple compiled list of questions to ask yourself to see if you've done the proper work needed to write a good one.

1. Who is in the scene?
2. Have you put a limitation on time? Where does this scene line up with that?

3. Where is the protag or antag trying to go?

Set pieces are action based, so don't get cute here, just write visually and show us what is happening. Be clear, concise, and simple, yet allow the tension and excitement to build. This should help diagnose set pieces that are too complex for their own good or if your script becomes sluggish.

Dialog

Now that you have fixed any structural issues and centered your characters, made sure they were acting consistently with their personalities, and doing their function, it is time to see what they are saying. The first moment your characters began to speak, it created a specific voice unique to them. This needs to stay consistent. Do they have pet phrases or a tonal way of speaking? This needs to stay consistent. When you pick up a phone you can tell who is speaking by their voice. You should be able to do this (within reason) from the page.

Expository dialog. Are your characters telling us what is going on? Remember that screenplays are visual, and your characters shouldn't be saying what they mean, but should mean what they say. Make sure you are not telling the story but showing it. I think less is more when it comes to dialog. Read each scene with the idea that you *can* cut some dialog. If you can't do without it, it stays. Does your dialog illuminate character? What your characters say informs the audience about their personalities. Remember Vinnie Jones's character the Sphinx in *Gone in 60 Seconds*? He had no lines until the end of the film and we knew everything we needed to; however, once he spoke it made him so much more. Think back on a film that you and your friends or family quote. My family still uses movie quotes from the '80s and '90s at the most hilarious moments during dinner. *Step Brothers* (Will Ferrell, Adam McKay) is one along with *Christmas Vacation* (John Hughes) and any Adam Sandler movie from the '90s. Chris Terrio said, "A good screenplay gives us memorable dialogue; but a great one gives us memorable silences." Look for the space between as much as the line.

One last thing about dialog. We have been trained since five years old to write with appropriate grammar. However, unless you are Kelsey Grammer's character Frasier, you don't speak with proper grammar (pun completely intended). Therefore you have to prepare to write incorrectly. Dialog got to be wrong to be right, or it's wrong. Right? Grammar is a tool that we writers use to get our point across in the most compelling way possible according to the character speaking. We don't work for grammar, grammar works for us. Be sure you are reading your dialog out loud. It really helps.

Grammar and Formatting

Are you writing in a visual way. Are you showing? Visual writing is a very different skill set, especially if you are coming from the creative writing world. Hopefully at this point you have read several good scripts and you understand how visual language is used in drama. As a matter of fact, there may not be a better way to learn dramatic writing than to read scripts and watch films. If you want to do this, you should be reading and screening the results—no excuses, do it. Everything on the page should show us something about the world or the characters. Concentrate on writing what shows up inside the lens of your mind. By this I mean literally imagine the scene in a little box (the camera). Show us that. We must assume that if it is on the page it is important. Don't forget tone either. The words that you use will resonate emotionally with people. You control that by being specific and intentional with the use of the words you use. Remember, no going inside the head of the protag, everything needs to be visual and dialog needs to be nonexpository.

Format is not an option. In screenwriting specific format is not used to decipher the difference between pros and amateurs, although it is immediately observable. Scripts are broken down by line producers by 1/8 of pages. Each 1/8 of a page generally costs a production twenty minutes of set time (barring action set pieces). Therefore, each page of a drama script takes two hours to shoot. If you mess up the formatting the production time can be off by considerable amounts. If the schedule is off, the budget is off, and this can cause a lot of damage. So, a good producer will chuck a badly formatted script due to the work it will take just to get it broken down properly. Buy a screenwriting program. There are many out there and some are free if you cannot afford the more expensive ones. Students and military often get a nice discount on products. I use Final Draft. It gives me everything I need without me having to focus on "how" to format. It is also the industry standard.

Formatting also means not directing on the page. CUT TO, MATCH CUT, ANGLE ON, THE CAMERA MOVES WITH, PAN, etc. These are not commands that writers generally use. These are for the director and cinematographer to inject after they have decided the aesthetics and shot list. As a writer, I do understand the frustration with losing control of your story; however, film-making is a collaborative art. Yes, a director can mess up your script. However, I tend to think that a director will have a hard time making a bad movie out of a good script. Usually when a director has a bad script they try to polish a turd and it comes out poorly. Do what is in your control. Write a great story and it will inspire greatness in others. Trust that a director wants to make your good script into a great movie. If you have control issues, think of it this way. If you sell your beloved car, once the paperwork is signed the car no longer belongs to you. A script is no different. When you sell it, and let's hope that you do, the product belongs to someone else. Be available to add value to the production any way you can, rather than add anxiety and unwanted advice.

Grammar. Many in the industry will tell you a single mistake in grammar gets your script thrown in the garbage. That is hogwash—yes, I said it again. I've read scripts that were amazing and had the same word misspelled twenty times. It was such a good story that I didn't notice. It is also true that some producers demand no grammar mistakes. Know your audience and get an editor. What I will say is this, grammar is there as a tool to help you tell your story well. You are not there to serve grammar, it is there to serve you. Use the language and tools within it to make compelling stories pop. A small mistake here or there won't affect you much if your story is well written. If your script sucks, grammar is an easy note for people to say NO to. You should also know that repeated mistakes can be annoying. If a grammar error impedes my ability as a reader to access the story, then it becomes an obstacle and problem. If you have a problem with grammar, find an editor. There is no shame in this. I had to pay an editor to work on my dissertation. It was a mess and academics tend to pay much more attention to grammar than readers. Work hard, proofread, know your audience, and/or hire an editor. Nobody passes on a script because the grammar was good.

Writers are unique in the filmmaking process as we are the only people who create from the abstract. You must understand that while there are tens of thousands of scripts making the rounds in Hollywood, perhaps 1 percent are good. Write well and you will be noticed. As Alfred Hitchcock said, "To make a great film you need three things, the script, the script, and the script."

CHAPTER 9

Weeks 15–16: Final Submission

Y ou've done all the hard work already. Well, kind of. Now that you have completed the next Oscar sleeper hit, where do you send it? You need to get eyes on it. Yes, this is also the hard part. In my master screenwriting class I give an assignment that asks students to do research on a studio or production company. The catch is that you have to find a company that makes movies like the one that you wrote. You can't send any script to any company. Now is the time to look up ten to fifteen movies in a genre and budget range that are similar to yours. You will see patterns emerge. Certain companies make certain types of movies within certain budget ranges. Write these down and find out everything you can about them. Who is the CEO, what spec deals they have they done, what is in development now, what is in production? What did their last three films do at the box office? You need to know everything you can about a company before you send them your script.

Now that you have a list of companies that you think are viable for your script, it is time to attack the how. Most companies do NOT accept unsolicited material. What does this mean? It means that they will not read your script unless they ask to read it. You can't email them and say, "Hey, I've got a great movie, just like XYZ that you made last year." They will delete your email without reading. This is not because they are mean. This is for legal purposes. If you have something close to what they have in development, it could cause issues, so they avoid it completely. You need an in. An agent, a manager, or lawyer can contact these companies on your behalf. That means you have to get representation, which opens up an entirely new set of questions, but I can't cover that here, because there is no one answer that works. You need to hit the bricks and reach out to lots of people. Writing groups are a good place not only to get valuable feedback on the scripts you're working on, but also as a place to build relationships for the future. A writing group friend who gets staffed is also a future networking connection. I have also noticed a lot of younger managers and junior agents more available on Twitter and Instagram lately. Scour all social media platforms that you can. Get a list of employees, what they do, their readers, friends of friends, etc. Networking is the name of the game now. You have to get to know someone. Sharpen up on your soft skills—they matter.

Let's get back to the writing and let's assume you have done the work and are nearly ready to submit. Your formatting is good, you've done a proofread. Let's talk about the polish. This is the very last thing you do before sending this out. Why? Once this gets in someone's hand, you never get that chance again. Hollywood, despite its mystique, is a very small place. Word gets around. You can't chance sending out subpar work. Once more into the breach, dear friends. Let's polish!

Here are four things to think about when polishing:

Deep and Rich: Dig Down

Is there any little component that you can add, a piece of more complex and fascinating material that would make things more interesting? For instance, in a script of mine I wrote a pretty nice character that hit all the marks. She was smart, flawed, active, and shy, and had a sibling rivalry. In the polish I decided to add a diagnosis of diabetes to her. This disease added an increased tension, an extra obstacle, and a more rich background to her history. For some reason it just made her that much more interesting. Obviously adding an autoimmune disease to every main character will NOT do the trick, but is there one more thing that makes someone stand out? This goes for plot and set pieces as well. Dig down into your imagination and pull out all the stops.

Character Polish

In chapter 8 we discussed how to get unstuck. Let's take one more look at your character(s), because it can be difficult to spot. Specifically I'm talking about behavior. Does your protag act like a real live human being?

Here are four quick hints to check.

1. Does you protagonist accept everything they hear and see as truth? Do they question absolutely nothing? If they stop to get gas at a bizarre little gas station and the weird attendant whispers that they should go

and check out the old house on Suspense Lane, will they thank them and go there? Humans don't usually act this way. Nor should any of your characters. Make them feel like real people.

2. Common sense. Does you protag act outside of how a normal human would react? A protag sees a hit-and-run and instead of calling 911, they follow the car into a dark alley and follow the driver into an underground rave club. WHAT? There is common behavior and acting outside of that is sometimes unbelievable. Unless you've set your character up to have no common sense, be careful here. Once again, make these people real.

3. Can the protag explain WHY they do what they are doing? There's a house fire and they barely escape, BUT the dog is stuck inside. I've got to save the dog, but the dog has not served a role in the film and we can't tell that they have a particular fondness for it. So WHY? Because it's a plot point. That answer doesn't work! Plausible explanations must accompany actions, and these actions should make sense based on their personality and past actions. Be consistent.

4. If things get rough, could your protag say, "EFF it" and go home? Remember that there needs to be a motivation and NEED that pushes the protag to accomplish their goal at ALL COSTS. If not, they can quit at any time and whatever stakes you have crumble. There needs to be a great cost for failure. Double down if you can.

Keep the Main Thing the Main Thing

I learned this when I was doing my doctoral research. When you start researching you can go down rabbit hole after rabbit hole. The trick is to stay focused on the research questions. Same goes for screenwriting. What is your premise? It should be taped above your computer and you should be looking at it all the time. If your third act is not answering the question of the premise (What if...?) and going in a different direction, something is wrong. Your story has to stay focused.

Here's an example. A story of a successful musician going down the drug drain to failure and destruction can't stray into a sudden interest in saving a town's economy, or finding inner peace though yoga ... *yes, this is a real script that failed.* The premise asks a question of your story, which is executed by the plot by way of choices resulting in actions by your protag. If any one of these are not happening, you have a problem. Full stop.

That about does it in my opinion. You've done the work. Be positive, be confident. Hit the send button on your submission and don't think twice about it. Do not follow up every week. Wait four to six weeks before contacting them again, unless you are instructed to do otherwise. Keep your emails short and to the point. These people receive a hundred emails per day. They don't have time to read a book. One or two sentences. Show them how concise you can be and be respectful of their time. Patience is the key. Don't sit and wait—start writing your next thing. You *always* need a next thing.

Pitch Deck

Okay, there is one more thing. You can put together a pitch deck. The entire film industry is predicated on screenplays, but almost no one in Hollywood ever reads. A conundrum to be sure. What to do? Build a pitch deck. A deck is a visual representation of your film's major components with minimal exposition. It will contain the one sheet (poster), a logline, tagline, and a synopsis at the minimum. Remember that a deck will set the tone visually. If you miss on tone or put together a shabby product, they will never read your script regardless of the script's quality. Do not send one of these out unless you know what you are doing and definitely not before you have seen several other decks. The benefit to a deck is that you can get the story, style, and pitch points of your script to a producer in a matter of minutes on *their* schedule. If they like it, they will get back to you. Production decks can be fifteen to twenty pages. I would recommend a script deck to be no more than eight to ten pages.

Page 1: The one sheet or poster. Make sure this poster tells the visual story of the script. The art needs to be good. The fonts easy to read. The tone needs to be felt. I would suggest a tagline, like a theater poster. Make the line short and snappy and memorable. It needs to look and feel like a movie.

Page 2: The logline. Make sure this tells us how the flawed protag has to DO something that leads to a conflict with an antagonist.

Pages 3–4: Synopsis. Summarize three acts. I would not use more than two pages for this. Be careful how much text you use on a single page. This needs to read well, but it also needs to LOOK good.

Page 5: Theme. This is optional, but I find it important to spell out to a producer the impact a theme has on the audience. I think it helps with the pitch and story.

Pages 6–7: Potential cast. I like to offer three actors for each main role. It gives the producers or marketing department a hint at what level the film should be made, as far as budget and distribution platform. If this goes, you most likely will get none of these actors, however, it helps with the pitch.

Page 8: Comparables. I find it helpful to find at least three films similar in budget, theme, genre, or plot. It is the new version of the pitch comp, "Clint Eastwood's *Drifter* meets *Independence Day.*"

Page 9: Contact info. This is an optional page, but I find it nice to have a bookend.

Remember that this deck is only for SELLING your script. It doesn't have to tell the entire story. It is an easy and effective way to get your script read.

There are many programs to build your deck. Some of these are available as freeware. Some of my students used Google Sheets and I was impressed. Some, however, looked very much like they used Google Sheets. I personally use Adobe Illustrator combined with Photoshop. These can be a bit pricey, but just like using a professional screenwriting program to keep things in their proper place, you don't want to look cheap. Appearances matter in this business. Look professional and invest in your own future to the extent that you can. I would even encourage you to seek out a graphic illustrator or designer. They have the requisite skills to make this nice. Last, you can't send this willy-nilly to anyone either. Same rules apply. Find a network and find a way in. If you have written a good script, chances are it will rise to the top like cream.

This is not an easy or forgiving industry; however, I have to say that I haven't yet found an industry where anything is a lay-up. Being a success in any industry requires study, work, practice, resilience, and a desire to do well. Yes, in Hollywood there are those who got a shot because of who they know or who they are related to, but if they suck first time out, they typically burn out. Nicholas Cage is a Coppola, but he is extremely gifted. Check out *Wild at Heart, Raising Arizona,* and *Mandy.* He earned his own stripes even if he was allowed to the front of the line. Imagine the world without him in film. Nepotism isn't unique to the film industry; it happens all over the world in every industry. Stay focused on what you have, not what you don't. Every producer, director, and actor wants to make an amazing film with critical success or sky-high profits, hopefully both. Write a great script. It's one of the only things in your control.

I want to wish you the greatest of success. Telling stories is a worthy career. It can truly affect people in positive ways. Work hard. Good luck.

FADE OUT.

CHAPTER 10

Adaptation

I decided to add this chapter because of how important I think adaptation is and because I believe it requires a skill set that differs from writing specs. The majority of features being produced today are sequels, prequels, or adaptations. The benefit of adaptation to a studio is that the primary source was good enough for publication, and therefore, it has already had one level of vetting. Second, the producers know the ending, which makes them feel in control. Last, these primary sources often have built-in audiences. This mitigates two problems for producers: First, they don't have to rely on a writer to provide a good ending, because they feel they have one already, and second, they may have financial data they can point to when pitching this to their bosses. Everyone in Hollywood is worried about their job in one way or another, and optioning an idea with intellectual property attached mitigates liability for them … at least that is what they think.

In our modern era, novels (novellas) and short stories are no longer the only sources of film adaptations. Graphics novels, comic books, video games, and news headlines are also sources of adaptation. It should also be mentioned that toys like G.I. Joe and cartoons like Looney Tunes have also been adapted. Due to the financially volatile nature of film, adaptations are vogue, and I foresee that it will stay that way.

With screenplays, everything must be on screen. There's no writing about what the character is feeling or thinking—you must show it through visuals, behavior, actions, and in dialog. Novels can explore the backstories and histories of your character and take fifty pages to do so. In a screenplay, your backstory must be woven into the current story or shown in a flashback that's less than four pages. A side note: I believe flashbacks are often lazy and unnecessary. If there is any way to avoid them, I would. Flashbacks can be useful and brilliant tools when deployed properly, however, it is often used as a crutch, which in my opinion hurts the work. Use every other tool you can before using a flashback. Novels can jump time periods easily and don't always have to be linear or structured. With screenplays, there should usually be a clear three-act structure, and there needs to be a really good reason for a screenplay to be told nonlinearly. There are many examples of films told in this unconventional way: *Pulp Fiction* and *Memento*, to name a couple. They are fantastic films, however, don't begin your project with the aim of telling it out of sequence; allow the story to tell you that it needs to be told this way.

With novels, you get a book jacket (or a mini synopsis on the back) that will tell you immediately if this is a book you want to read. With screenplays this isn't the case, so it's the first ten pages or so that must grab your reader or else they won't read any further.

A book is a book and a film is a film. They are different, and we should understand this from the get. Most novels and short stories (or other sources) need something to turn them into good films. A good book does not a good film make. One may look through the impressive repertoire of Stephen King and pick out any number of films that did not meet muster, despite being good reads. If a good Stephen King novel can't always be a good movie, what gives? Remember that these are different media told in different ways. Good story is always the core, but a good story needs to be completely visual or it won't play.

Now that you know some of the differences, how do you actually start the adaptation process? Let's start broadly and get more specific as we go. I will lay out what I believe is a firm scaffolding to preparing a source for adaptation. Here are a few hints to start.

1. Read the damn book! Don't skim. Read it. First, it is respectful, and second you need to understand why this story has been optioned. You can't write what you don't know. No guessing—read it.
2. If the original author is alive, see if you can get hold of them to talk. They know this story better than you ever will. If you can discuss it with them, they will be a great source of the nuanced things that may not be evident to you in the source. Take notes and be specific. Something might come in very handy.
3. Do not be afraid to Create a new Original. Be bold and don't feel as if you are not allowed to change what needs to be changed to make a movie. Stephen King and Michael Crichton are great writers, but their books can't be transcribed into films. Here's a quote from J. Hart: "When I read a book, I know that the narrative is too long for a film

adaptation. The writer's mission is to create a new original that honors the intention and the spirit of the original." Your film may have to tell a slightly different story from a different point of view to make it visually engaging enough to make a good film.

Now we prepare the new original by making some decisions. You have read or examined the source closely, potentially spoken with the original author, and been able to discover the core essence of the piece. This is the spirit of the work, and this is what we begin with.

Eight Steps

1. The Spirit

To approach adaptation, we all must sit back and decide as writers what we feel is the spirit of the story. This central idea, theme, emotion, message—however you define it—is the core of the story. This spirit is what you as the writer must stay true to, not the pages themselves. I say this as an author of a novel (yes, I wrote a book, *The Virus Chronicles: The Culling*), not as a screenwriter with eager hedge trimmers bent on cutting a novel to its quick. A film requires different visual elements to move its plot along and some novels do not have this visual element. Find the spirit of the book (source), what the author means to say, and stay true to that. Find that core element that makes their book special and unique. It is to that core that you must stay true. To stay true to the core, you may need to change a few things. Okay, metaphor time.

Henry Eckford built some of the best ships in the U.S. Navy. There is no question that he was a master builder and an expert on surface transportation. If we were to adapt his "floating on the water" idea to a "floating on the clouds" idea, we would have to change a few things around. Boats just don't fly, especially in 1812. It sounds simple doesn't it? Boats don't fly and novels don't make good films without change. Find the spirit and stick to it.

2. Tension

Most people aren't cognizant to the fact that what holds their attention in movies is tension. For a script to hold water, it needs two types of tension. Let's start on the inside. Internal tension is an exploitation of a problem or flaw unique to the character, and that character is affected directly by the choices they make in concert with these issues. The results of these choices are tension and conflict. In Stephen King's *It*, we see one of the characters is an extremely violent bully. He causes tension in the film, but ultimately, we find that he is an abused child and that this is his internal struggle. That struggle is exploited by the pervasive evil of the town and presents him as a bully. The bully's character makes choices that result in incredible amounts of tension resulting in conflict for the other characters. Tension holds the entire thing together. In a novel or similar primary source, internal tension can be explored in and out of a character's brain. We can sit with them and listen simultaneously to their conversation, as well as their internal debate. We can explore the depths of thought, guilt, pride, arrogance, etc. How can we have this same type of tension on screen? We need to see this debate, not be told about it. The trick is to find the tension that already exists in the source or to create a tension that fits naturally within the story. You need internal struggle to make this work, so don't let this pass by without any thought.

It is important to remember that internal tension is a DIRECT cause of the CHOICES of the character. It is my personal belief that when it correlates with the theme it resonates more strongly. We discussed theme in chapter 4. There must be consequences to the choice derived from the internal tension. Think about the stakes here. The better the tension, the better you will hook your audience. Internal tension directly affects the main character and is an absolute must, even in comedies. Find these internal idiosyncrasies and imagine how they would LOOK and how you could use them to create obstacles, develop character, and identify solutions for your character.

In a sentence, internal tension is often emotional, academic, intellectual, and personal. It is a fight we can't see unless as writers we show it on purpose. Some sources will lay these ideas out for you. I do not think you need to reinvent the wheel if they do. Again, stay true to the core, and if the answers are presented in the source, use them.

External tension is a global situation that affects all the characters equally (good and bad). Most often this is what is referred as the ticking clock, although it is not always so. In the movie *2012*, the imminent destruction of the Earth is the external tension. It carries out and pushes the movie forward. The internal tension was the divorced couple. External tension is that thing that looms in the background and will have to be dealt with. It will change the way all the characters move forward.

External tension ups the stakes by suggesting worst-case outcomes and makes resolution vital (the protagonist must overcome the antagonist/environment) or everyone dies (a bit hyperbolic, I know). It also forces character development. Conflict allows for dramatic incidents and confrontations that test characters and push them to change one way or another.

Let's combine internal and external tension to see how they work together to keep an audience engaged.

A KING is brutally slain by his best FRIEND, who then claims the throne. The son of the slain KING, the PRINCE, is now seeking revenge and to take back the crown for his family and country; however, the FRIEND has also kidnapped the old KING's daughter, PRINCESS, and uses her as leverage against the impending battle. Let's break this down.

*ENTER INTERNAL CONFLICT: The PRINCE is advised to act in a measured way and accept the new King, and that vengeance will destroy the kingdom. What internal issues does the son have? Was he loved, is he weak, does the Senate control him as a puppet, was he secretly in love with his sister? Would he rather NOT be king? The choices that the PRINCE makes based on the internal struggle will create internal tension, loads of it! His choices, good or bad, all add to the mix and the audience is sucked in.

*ENTER EXTERNAL CONFLICT: Unbeknownst to either of them, is an EVIL that has lain dormant for centuries. This ancient evil has awoken and is creeping toward the kingdom to overtake it as legend and prophecy have foretold. Here is a curve ball. The antagonist (the KING's best FRIEND, who killed him) was raised by a brutal religious sect and hates the Priests. Therefore, he does not believe in the prophecy. So he does not pay any mind to the external tension.

1. The PRINCE is in secret love with his sister, PRINCESS, and is bent of getting her back. He will burn the entire kingdom to do so.
2. The NEW King doesn't believe in religious hogwash and ignores the threats.

*DO YOU SEE HOW THIS TRANSLATES VISUALLY? We explore the internal struggle ON screen, not in the character's heads. Depending on your primary source, a conflict like this may need to be created. Remember Leo DiCaprio's character Hugh Glass in The Revenant. Most of the novel is a struggle within Glass's mind, but onscreen we can't have him lay on the ground for ninety minutes. A son and wife were invented to provide a source of internal struggle and motivation for him. Imagine how that movie would have felt if it was about a dude who was so pissed his friends left him for dead that he sought revenge. A little bit of a different tone than what they did and potentially not an Oscar winner.

Back to our example. The betrayal of the KING blinds the PRINCE. The lust for power and lack of reflection blinds the FRIEND, and looming battle overshadows the greatest threat (external tension), which is the coming of the ancient EVIL. Due to the actions of the protag and antag, the kingdom might be lost forever. Will the two sides join forces to stop the evil and save the kingdom? Needle drop suspense music here! This is the power of external tension combined with internal.

External tension is the main conflict, and it is an absolute must, even in comedies. Hopefully, the source material you are adapting has all these elements already, but they may not, because they may not need to. You have to design these symmetrically opposite tension(s) to push a visual story forward, as well as keep the audience interested in the characters and their relationships. Lindsay Doran, a spectacular script consultant, focuses much of her advice on writing good films on the basis of relationships within the movie. Relationships are a mechanism of internal tension, which is tested by the external tension. External conflicts are usually between a character and external forces; between one character and another or a group (or between groups of characters). It can also be between a character and more abstract forces, like a bleak and hostile environment in a postapocalyptic novel or a hurricane. External tension affects everyone.

"Sir Thomas felt deeply in his heart that the lady was no good. The thought of her, however, stirred his loins and he had a hard time getting her out of his mind. He knew one day she might be his down fall and the ruin of his marriage."

How would a director film this? How would you write it to actually SHOW something? I know what you are thinking; VOICE OVER! NOOOOO! If this is essential to the plot, you should think of how to SHOW it. If you are stuck, I would suggest perhaps taking a character from the source or creating one to allow the protagonist to vent. This type of information should create tension, but not be expository or it will come off as stupid and trite.

Tension is not difficult to write for those screenwriters that use a solid framework for structure (chapter 4), but for those that put pen to paper without any planning it can be more of a challenge. Tension is a pervasive device, and the thing that keeps the audience watching and the reader reading.

Remember it needs to be both in and out. TV writers are great at keeping us on the edge of our seats (think *Lost*). Search for the obvious forms of both types of tension in the source or create ways that feel most natural.

Quickly recapping, we have read the novel fully, maybe even spoken with the original author. We have established what we believe is the spirit or core of the novel. That spirit is what we believe the original author wanted to say and we have dedicated ourselves to holding true to that spirit for as far as we can to deliver a good film. Second, we identified within the source two types of tension, internal and external. If we did not find good enough examples, we have begun to brainstorm ways to make the tension work within the spirit of the source. Now to the third step.

3. Setting

I am sure the setting in the original source is clear, but your adaptation does not have to happen in the same world, universe, or time that the primary source material happens, especially if you are using a headline, for instance. Due to the difference in media there may be a better or more interesting VISUAL way to tell a story. Earlier I said not to reinvent the wheel. If the setting is good then don't change, but don't feel anchored to it either. This is an important decision for you to make and one that must serve the story. Ask yourself:

Is the spirit of the novel (story) tied to the setting?
Is there a more exciting way to tell this story?
Where? When? Why?

Modern remakes of William Shakespeare plays are a good example of setting and time shifts: the 1996 *Romeo + Juliet* (Pierce, Luhrmann) and *The Lion King* (Mecchi, Roberts, Woolverton) based on Hamlet.

4. Characters

We discussed all things character in previous chapters (chapters 5 and 6). Most of the characters you come across in a primary source will already be developed; however, you will need to assign functional roles to them. Screenplays require more efficiency in characters than novels. List five to eight main characters of the story, including protagonist and antagonist. What are their respective backstories and how/why do they come together? As we have already discussed, try to assign functions for your characters to be sure your plot can be realized. Keep in mind here that you can cut or create characters as needed or even combined them. Ask yourself these questions:

Whose story is it?
What do they want?
Who wants to stop them?
Who wants to help them the most? Why?
Is there a difference between protag and narrator/POV?
Is there a better person to tell this story? For example, Bram Stoker's *Dracula* adaptation was not a story about Dracula, but Mina Murray.

Will audiences accept the characters as written in the original? For example, In *Tuck Everlasting* (novel), Winnie (love interest) was ten years old and Jesse was seventeen. How would audiences have dealt with the obvious age disparity between a very young girl and a character who was nearly a fully grown man in a film?

5. Pertinent Information

Make a list of five things from your primary source about your protagonist and your antagonist that the audience should know. This will most likely show up in the first ten pages of your screenplay, so you need to how you will show these. This is assuming that your primary source is not a toy with the only important feature being a Kung Fu grip.

6. Visual Conflict

What is the major conflict (external tension)? Good news, you should already know this from earlier. What is that one moment at the tip of Freytag's triangle that garners the most tension in the book? How and why does this occur? How can you SHOW this conflict unfold? Keep in mind that identifying conflict is wildly important, but in this step it needs to be visually apparent for it to work on a screen. In film, the major conflict is many times a failure on the part of the protagonist, which they must come back from.

7. Favorite Scenes

When my friend Vince McKewin (*Replacements, Fly Away Home*) and I were adapting my novel, *The Virus Chronicles: The Culling*, he said someone he knew gave him good advice about adapting. "Get two copies of the book. Every time you come across a scene that you like or think is important, tear the page out and lay it on the floor. When you are done, you can arrange the scenes anyway you want to." A literature puzzle. That's awesome. I sent him two copies of the book. With that in mind you should identify scenes that you absolutely love, think are important, and/or most visually connect to how the story unfolds. These are big moments: emotional, physical, psychological, etc. This could be ten to fifty scenes, and each scene may not end up in the script, but ten should be the minimum. Do not short yourself.

8. Dialog

Jot down your ten to twenty favorite lines of dialog that drive the plot and are vital to the story or character development. Yes, you may jot down others as well. I would suggest separate lists that identify plot-driving dialog, character development dialog, and just straight-up cool dialog that is sharp, witty, and memorable. A line from *Mandy* comes to mind, when Red says, "You are a vicious snowflake." Yeah, a line like that. It makes people go, "ooohhh." Thanks for taking this gig, Nick Cage.

Let's recap. We read and explored the source material and if we could we spoke to the original author, which is a way for us to identify what we feel is the spirit of the novel (source). Then we identified two types of tension: internal and external. With this information we have to make a decision on setting and character, articulate pertinent information about these characters, identify the conflict, choose our favorite (most important) scenes, and select the best lines of dialog. With all this information right in front of us, we can begin putting together a screenplay. Go back to chapter 2 and begin preparation. Wash, rinse, repeat.

You may be asking yourself, is this the way you do adaptation? The answer is yes ... and no. There is no ONE WAY, only your way. There are really no rules to this. The above is a schematic of *A* way of organizing material and getting all the necessary information into a film script. These are suggestions and you should always try to find a way that does the above, but is most comfortable for you. The way your brain works and integrates with creativity is unique to you. The process can be ugly and messy, but as long as the results are good, who cares. The only thing that matters in the end is a good screenplay.

FADE OUT.

Answers to Exercises

Exercise #1

Sling Blade

Story: A simple-minded man bonds with a young boy, becoming his protector.

Plot: A man is released from a mental institution where he was committed for the murder of his father and returns to his hometown.

The Godfather

Story: A man takes over the family business after his father dies.

Plot: A mob war over heroin and the assassination attempt of the Boss (father). The son, Michael, who has stayed away, chooses to assassinate another mob boss and goes to Italy to hide, beginning his ascension into the ranks.

CPSIA information can be obtained
at www.ICGtesting.com
Printed in the USA
LVHW021458120123
736951LV00003B/714

9 781469 674261